Secret Garden of Survival™

Do you think you are prepared for the next big disaster?
What are you going to eat when food stores run out?
How do you keep others from taking it?

How to Grow a Camouflaged Food Forest

THE SURVIVALIST GARDENER

Copyright © 2012-2014 Rick Austin, The Survivalist Gardener™

All rights reserved.

ISBN-10: 1481839772
ISBN-13: 9781481839778

DEDICATION

This book is dedicated to all those people, everywhere, who wish to take responsibility for their own welfare, and for the welfare of their families. Whether you call yourself a homesteader, a "prepper", a survivalist, or something else, this book will help those of you who wish to be self-sufficient, to be able to provide an abundant supply of good healthy food for yourself and your family, in good times and in bad.

CONTENTS

	Forward	i
1	What Do I Know About This?	1
2	Starting with a Clean Slate	13
3	Grey Water Systems	19
4	Swales, Irrigation, Micro-Climates	24
5	Permaculture Guilds	30
6	Rain Water Collection	35
7	Vegetable and Herb Garden	39
8	Infrastructure for the Garden	42
9	Preparing the Ground	57
10	Planting Your Food Forest	68
11	Observing and Improving Natural Pest Control	80
12	Growing Through The Season	89
Bonus	What To Do After The Harvest	98
	Conclusion	108

THE SURVIVALIST GARDENER

FORWARD:

Studies of native indigenous people around the world (people who have lived off the land for generations without electricity, without refrigeration, without commercial agriculture, and without pesticides and insecticides) showed that these people have lived primarily on perennials (plants that grow year after year without replanting) as opposed to annuals such as your typical grocery store vegetables (crops that you must replant each year).

Aside from living off perennial fruits and nuts, these indigenous people also lived on small animal proteins …In other words, people who have survived for generations, without the modern day comforts of a consumer society, have done so by eating fruits and nuts from the land, as well as small animals - (rabbits, birds, fish, etc.)

In a future world where there is potentially no electricity, no refrigeration, no super markets, no seed stores, no fertilizers, no pesticides and no feed stores (for domestic farm animals), it makes sense to look at people who have managed to live successfully for generations without these "conveniences".

Furthermore, these people are simply "hunter/gatherers"- so instead of spending their time planting and tending crops, these people spend the majority of their time harvesting their food, without all the "work" that you would typically think of with traditional gardening.

These people don't plant in rows, they don't plant year after year, they don't weed, they don't fertilize, and they don't water plants in order for the plants to survive long enough to bear fruit.

Yet they have managed to survive for hundreds, if not thousands of years this way…

If you keep this thought in mind while reading this book, you'll understand that you can create your own "Garden of Eden", which works with nature, instead of against it. A garden that provides you with more and better food than you could ever imagine, with less work than any garden you have ever planted before. And perhaps most important of all, your garden will be disguised to look like "nature", so that no one would ever assume you had food planted there.

CHAPTER 1
WHAT DO I KNOW ABOUT THIS?

I used to be a traditional apple farmer. And just like every other traditional apple farmer, I had acres of apple trees planted in rows and rows, with nothing but grass growing in between.

And just like every other traditional apple farmer, I spent a fortune on fertilizer and pesticide - every 10 days and also after every rain. Yet I still had wormy, scabby apples, just like every other farmer around me.

Asian Pears - grown in a food forest, without pesticide or fertilizer

Little did I know then that the grass in between the trees sucked up the same nutrients that the apple trees needed. And little did I know then that the pesticide I was using was actually making my apples a bigger target for the pests I was trying to get rid of. That is because the predator bugs that would have taken care of the pests, were dying from the pesticide faster than the pests!

Aside from having been a farmer, I have also been a "survivalist" and a "prepper" -- long before they coined the terms.

Living for years in New Hampshire as I did, I learned how to prepare for and survive hard winters, where on any given day, a blizzard or ice storm could leave you without power for a week at a time. When that happens, you learn the importance of knowing how to heat and cook with wood, the importance of keeping plenty of storage food on hand, and the fundamentals of surviving the elements without power.

On the flip side, I also lived for years in Florida in the hurricane, tropical storm and lightning capital of the world. There, when the power is out, instead of freezing temperatures, you find yourself coping with 90+ degree heat and 90% humidity. And without power, computers, TV, refrigeration and air conditioning, life can be tough.

Aftermath of Hurricane Sandy (AP Photo)

Living through the aftermath of storms, with home damage, down trees, blocked roads, closed stores, empty gas stations, and the inability to use credit or debit cards at stores, makes you realize that you have to be prepared, and that you have to be self-reliant- because no one is coming to save little old you, when everyone is in the same boat.

Consequently, you learn to prepare by having adequate food storage, alternate means of cooking, cleaning, backup power, home protection, and ways to "light up the night".

So - are you prepared for the next disaster? - Just what kind of disasters are you prepared for?

Well, the truth is that it really doesn't matter if it is a hurricane, a flood, an earthquake, a blizzard, or an economic collapse - the results will ultimately be the same. There will be no electricity, no water, no food, no infrastructure, no grocery stores, no gas stations, and after a short time, social anarchy will ensue, with every man for himself and the zombie hordes attacking anyone that has anything they might want, in order to feed themselves and their own family.

Zombie hordes approaching by sea. (AP Photo)

So how are you prepared? Do you have a bug out bag? Do you have a place to shelter? Do you have preparations for your home and your family's defense?

How much food do you have in storage? A few days? A few weeks? A few months? A year or more?

If there are no grocery stores, no infrastructure, and no government to help you, how are you going to feed yourself and your family in times of catastrophe - whether that is short term or long term?

Less than 100 years ago, the average family always had a year's worth of food saved in storage to last them until the next harvest.

Aside from food storage, have you considered keeping homestead food producing animals? Chickens, ducks, goats, rabbits can all provide that small animal protein that we talked about in the Forward of this book.

Additionally these type of animals yield a high amount of protein verses their input. In other words, these small animals give you more output per pound of feed, in less space, than other sources of protein, like cattle an dairy cows do.

These small animals also provide valuable nitrogen rich nutrients in the form of manure, that will help your plants grow, giving you more feed for yourself, and for your animals.

Small homestead animals are a valuable source of protien

As an aside, I prefer ducks over chickens, in that ducks produce more eggs, are generally healthier than chickens, and they travel the garden eating bugs and slugs, without digging up your tender plants (like chickens do when scratching).

People all over the world use dairy goats for milk, cheese, yogurt and other protein rich products.

OK - So let's say you survive TEOTWAWKI ("The End Of The World As We Know It") …and let's say that you even survive for a whole year…

What are you and your livestock going to eat when your food stores run out?

How will you replenish a year's supply of food storage, and then continue to feed yourself and your animals each and every year after that?

And how will you keep other people, who didn't bother to prepare, from stealing your family's food, when those unprepared people become a hungry, angry mob?

Imagine a food garden that you only have to plant once in your lifetime, that takes up very little space, that will provide food for you and your family for the next 30 years; that can grow five times more food per square foot than traditional or commercial gardening; where you never have to weed, never have to use fertilizers and never have to use pesticide -- ever.

And the whole garden is disguised to look like overgrown underbrush, so that anyone passing by would not even dream that you had food growing there!

What it is...

-I call type of gardening **Nature-Culture™** where you **let nature do what nature does best**...the way nature intended it. - And as you will see later in this book, when man thinks he can do something better than nature does it, he usually screws it up.

-In many ways this type of garden uses the concept of "Permaculture" (or "permanent agriculture"). In this type of garden, you, as the gardener, only have to **plant once - and a then you harvest for a lifetime**.

-In this type of garden you **plant in "guilds" instead of rows**. Guilds are like concentric circles of plants planted around the central plant of the guild, such as a fruit or a nut tree. Your shrubs are then planted around your tree, and your herbs are planted around your shrubs and ground cover is planted around that. (We will get into more detail in Chapter 5.)

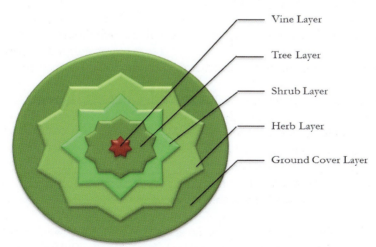

Layers of a Guild- (Top Down View)

-This type of garden also uses **"companion planting"**, where you put plants together that have a symbiotic relationship - a relationship where each plant supports and benefits from the other. (If you have ever heard of the book *Carrots Love Tomatoes*, it's like that, only on a much larger scale.)

-This type of garden uses plants to naturally attract **"good bugs" that will pollinate your plants and that will also prey on and kill the "bad bugs"** that you don't want in your garden.

-This type of garden **uses plants to keep away four legged pests** too. For example, if you plant onions around the base of a fruit tree, mice won't go near the tree in the winter and gird it. ("Gird" is where an animal chews off the bark around the bottom of the tree, thus killing the tree.) Likewise, if you plant daffodils around the drip line of a tree, deer won't go near it.

-This type of garden **grows plants in three dimensions** - so you can put more plants in the same area, which will significantly increases the amount of food you produce per square foot of garden space. (In fact, you can grow 5X more food per square foot in this type of garden, than you could in a traditional row garden.)

-Not only can you grow more plants in less space, **but the individual plants grow better this way** too! For example: In nature, vines grow on trees (not on trellises). Amazingly, the grape vines that we planted next to, and have growing on, our fruit trees, have always produced far more grapes than those vines that we planted on traditional vineyard trellises.

2 year old grapes growing on an apple tree

2 year old grapes growing on a trellis

-This type of garden looks wild and over grown - and just like the art of camouflage - it all blends in. Because it **has no definable shapes or rows. It looks "natural", not man-made.**

What it is not…

    -**It's not work** - because once you are finished with your initial planting, all you do is harvest, year after year.

    -**It's not weeding** - In this garden; you don't have to pull weeds. …Because for the most part, weeds are good. You see, weeds are just misunderstood plants. Weeds are "pioneer" plants, because they are generally the first plants to inhabit a new area. As such, they serve a purpose. Weeds will grow where other plants could not survive, and in the meantime, their roots break up hard packed soil so that water,

microorganisms and other nutrients can move in. Additionally, when the weeds die, they create compost and mulch that will help other plants to be able to take over where they left off.

For example: have you ever looked at a newly clear cut field or the edge of a forest? Weeds are the first to move in...Then, over time, the lifecycle continues, so that herbs can grow, then shrubs (like blue berries and blackberries), and eventually trees and vines can move in. (This is the life cycle of a forest - from weeds and grasses to herbs and shrubs, to short softwood trees like pines, to tall hardwood trees like oaks.)

In this close up photo of our Secret Garden of Survival, there are bush beans, cucumbers, peanuts, passion fruit, comfrey, mint, mountain mint, clover and oats- all growing in the same space...And all of this is underneath a pear tree that stands next to blueberry bushes. (Can you find them all?)

-It's not using pesticide - You need to understand this simple fact: 90% of all bugs are "good bugs". Good bugs are beneficial insects that in one way or another are essential to the growth and health of your plants. Unfortunately, most insecticides do not discriminate, so they not only kill the bad bugs that you want to eliminate, but they also kill the beneficial insects as well. By killing the good bugs, you interrupt the lifecycle of the predator bugs, and then you leave your plants vulnerable to numerous other pests, that you didn't even know could be a problem.

Furthermore, once you have killed the predator bugs that were protecting your plants, the "bad bugs" can invade at will, and then your garden suddenly becomes a smorgasbord without anyone there to protect it.

Additionally, these pesticides end up in the soil and they can kill the good microorganisms that allow your plants to be able to take up nutrients.

Nature has its own way of keeping things in balance. When you interfere with nature's balance by using chemical pesticides, you end up creating an even bigger problem for yourself and your plants – and- you could end up with no crops at all...

This type of garden looks wild and over grown, because it all blends in.

Even worse, some of these pesticides are systemic. In other words, once they end up in the soil they can then be absorbed throughout the entire system of your plant. So your plants will then carry these pesticides through their roots, into their stems, into their leaves, and into their pollen, thus killing even more good bugs. And if you can ever get fruit to grow under these conditions, these pesticides will now be inside of the food you are going to eat.

Lastly - where do you think you are going to get pesticide when the grid goes down anyway? When there are no stores, and no transportation, there will be no commercial pesticide available. It is far better to never start using them.

-It's not using fertilizer - In nature, plants grow just fine without commercial fertilizer. Yet almost all commercial farming, and most residential gardens, rely on it. The problem is that using commercial fertilizer is a lot like giving your plants addictive drugs...and once they are addicted, they have a hard time living without it.

And just like pesticide above, where are you going to get commercial fertilizer after TEOTWAWKI (The End Of The World As We Know It)?

...By the way, since the day we started our Secret Garden of Survival, we have never used one single ounce of pesticide or one single once of fertilizer on our plants, and we have always had more food than we could possibly consume.

-It's not watering- Once your plants are established, there is little to no need for watering in the Secret Garden of Survival. That is because the best place to store water for your garden is in the ground.

In permaculture, we use swales (berms and terraces) to store water. (See the illustration below.) When water drains down into the terrace, it is stopped from flowing further down-hill by the berm on the terrace. The water then seeps into the ground. A lens shaped pool of water forms under the berm. This water is available to the roots of the plants on the berm.

During droughts, when everyone else's plants were dying, our plants where healthy and green. (For more info see Chapter 4 on Swales, Irrigation, and Micro Climates.)

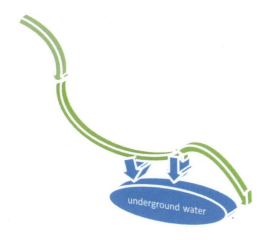

Swales slow downhill water flow creating an underground pool for your plants.

(Later in this book we will discuss how you can use grey water (Chapter 3) and rain water collection (Chapter 6) to supplement water for your plants (and animals).

So to sum up, The Secret Garden of Survival is a garden that takes up very little space, that you only have to plant once in your life-time, that will provide food for you and your family for the next 30 years; that can grow five times more food per square foot than traditional or commercial gardening; and it's a garden that you never have to weed, never have to use fertilizers and never have to use pesticide-- ever.

Here is an example of how well it works. It amazes even me. In 2 years- we went from red clay to 12 ft. high blackberries, 15 ft. fruit trees that were bearing fruit, and a lush green food forest that passers-by could not recognize as a "garden".

We went from red clay terraces to 12' high blackberries in just 2 years.

We went from red clay to a lush food forest in just two years.

Now that you know the basics of what it is, and why it works, want to find out HOW YOU can do this?

Then read on…

CHAPTER 2
STARTING WITH A CLEAN SLATE

We started our Secret Garden of Survival by clearing less than half an acre of mature oak forest on the south facing side of a hill.

If I had to pick an ideal situation for a Secret Garden of Survival, it would be on top of a hill, with a ¼ acre (or more) of land, cleared on the south side (south facing is best for solar), with a house on top of that hill and the permaculture garden down below (for gravity flow of grey water and rainwater collection cisterns to use for garden irrigation).

Now you may be working with existing property that you already own. So your situation will probably be different than the ideal. The permaculture concept will still work, but the closer you are to the ideal clean slate, the better it will work for you.

Solar Path- One of the key things to consider in establishing a new Secret Garden of Survival is the garden's placement in relation to the sun.

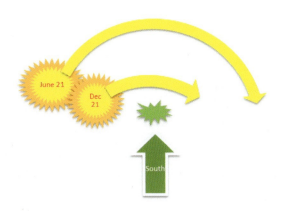

Planting on the south side of a property gives the longest growing season.

The sun rises in the east and sets in the west and travels across the southern sky during the day (in the northern hemisphere anyway). The sun is higher in the sky in the summer (so more direct and stronger –thus hotter) and the sun is lower in the sky in the winter time (thus less direct and weaker). Therefore planting on the south side of your property will be best for most plants and give you a longer growing season. And since it is warmer sooner in the spring and warmer later in the fall, not only will you have a longer growing season, but early frosts in both spring and fall will have less negative impact on your plants.

Because the sun rises in the east and sets in the west, having tall trees on either side of your garden will mean that your garden's west side will have more morning sun, with afternoon shade, whereas on the east side, you will have morning shade, with intense afternoon sun. And of course the center of your garden will be getting sun all the time.

This is important when it comes time to consider what you are planting and where. Some plants like afternoon sun, some like morning sun, and some need only a few hours of direct sunlight, some plants like shade, and some need full and direct sun all day long. Thus, you will need to determine what you plant and where, accordingly.

Here is one example of specialized placement for certain plants…Many apple trees, need a certain number of "chill hours" (hours at or below 45 degrees each winter season) before they will 'activate' and set blossoms and thus set fruit. In this case, if you live in a more temperate climate (zone 7 or higher) (see zone map of the US below) you may want to plant some of these trees on the north side of your property. Keep in mind that in order to make the guilds work, you will also need to plant companion plants in that guild that can work with those additional chill hours.

The USDA has a Plant Hardiness map with Zones to help you determine the best plants for your climate.

Clearing the Land- If you are clearing the area for your garden from an established forest, save the lumber that you clear from the lot. A local saw mill can mill and kiln-dry the softwood (i.e. pine) for you to use as building material (for your use in the construction of your various buildings). We used our softwood lumber to build a summer kitchen, as well as parts of our barn.

You can then sell the hardwood (i.e. oak) for cash. This is because unless you are a master craftsman and want to create your own cabinets or flooring, hardwood is difficult to work with in the building process.

Sell or mill your good lumber to use for building on your property.

Save your scrap wood for use as nutrients under your berms.

Save the scrap wood (the trees and branches that are not so thick and not so straight), in other words, the wood that would be useless for milling, and use those trees and branches under your berms. This scrap wood will be decomposition material that will provide nutrients to feed your plants that you put on your berms.

You can also use some of the not-so-perfect logs to propagate mushrooms. You can buy plugs of various types of mushrooms to "inoculate" your logs, so that you can grow specific types of mushrooms of your choosing.

Use some of your not-so-perfect lumber to propagate mushrooms.

Because mushrooms are difficult to identify, and because so many are toxic, it is best to use this inoculation method, so that you will know what you are growing, without question.

Once you have the trees cleared from the garden area, you will need to remove the stumps. Leaving the roots in place is OK for now. We will discuss this in more detail in Chapter 8.

Once you have a clean slate, you can get started with the "infrastructure" for your garden.

CHAPTER 3
GREY WATER SYSTEMS

What is grey water? What is black water?

Simply put, the term "grey water" is used to describe all the water going down the drain in your house, except for the water used to remove toilet waste. Toilet waste water is called "black water".

So- all the water that you use to shower, wash your hands, and even do the dishes, is considered grey water.

And this grey water can amount to a lot of water- 200 or more gallons per day for a family of two.

Grey water can be reclaimed and used to flush toilets, and for our purposes, it can also be used to water your garden and greenhouse plants.

A grey water *system* can be as simple as a washing machine's laundry drain hose running into an exterior 55 gallon drum. If the drum has a spigot at the bottom, you can then attach a garden hose to water the plants in your garden.

Even though you could put grey water from the laundry right onto the ground around your plants, if you use hot water to do your laundry, then that hot water could effectively scald your roots and harm the vital soil organisms in the garden. So the idea behind using a 55 gallon drum is simply to allow the hot water to cool in the drum *before* draining it directly onto your berms, and your plant roots.

A simple grey water system drains water from your washer into your garden.

    Contrary to what you might think, most laundry detergents can be used directly on the ground, and many contain nutrients that your plants can use. The only thing to avoid here are detergents that contain chlorine/bleach, or detergents that are particularly high in salts, which could end up killing roots and plants. It is also best to be able to move your hoses periodically, so that you are not dumping these detergents on the same spot all the time…and so that one area is not always wet- to avoid root rot.
    A grey water system can also be as complex as a whole house grey water system, where the grey water and the black water in a home are separated (using separate drains) and where that grey water can be diverted from the home into a man-made wet land.
    Man-made wetlands are used commercially all over the planet. They clean water naturally by using plants and microorganisms, and the grey water in turn, provides nutrients for other sources of food for you and your animals (i.e. cat tails, and other crops).

    Once in that wetland, the water can then go through a series of baffles, thus slowing the water flow and letting the plants and microorganisms in the wet land work to clean the water, before it travels on in your system.

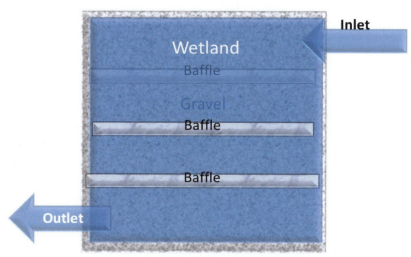

Grey water goes into a gravel wetland, past baffles and out to ponds.

If set up correctly, by the third day, your house water should be clean and can flow into trickle ponds (to aerate the water) which can then flow into a bigger pond, for use by fish, ducks, and aquatic plants (that you can eat too) such as water cress, water chestnuts, and duckweed- (a high protein crop).

Grey water from the home flows into a wetland, trickle pools and duck pond.

The pond should also be set up so that it can be drained with pipes and valves in order to water your crops if there are long periods between rain falls. And since this pond water will have additional nitrogen rich nutrients from fish and duck waste, the water will be even better for your plants. (If it smells "fishy" it's good for the plants!)

Junction box connecting 2" drain from pond to garden hose drains.

If at all possible, it is preferable to have your pond at a higher elevation than your garden, so that the water can be gravity fed into your garden, without the use of pumps or electricity.

A word of caution here: You need to be even more careful with the use of detergents, chlorine bleach and other chemicals going down your drains into this system than you would have been with a simple grey water laundry system; since certain chemicals can kill the ecosystem (fish, tadpoles, etc.) in your pond. Simple soaps are OK to use in this system, but chemical cleansers for sinks, bathtubs, etc. are probably not a good idea.

By the way- vinegar is one of the greatest, organically safe cleansers there is- and you can make it yourself, simply by further fermenting cider, or wine, that you can make from the apples or grapes in your permaculture survival garden.

Simply put, reclaiming your grey water in this way can give you an extra 200- 300 gallons of water/day to water crops that would have otherwise been wasted going into a sewer system, or septic tank.

SECRET GARDEN OF SURVIVAL

CHAPTER 4
SWALES, IRRIGATION, MICRO-CLIMATES

As we discussed in Chapter One, swales, berms and the like help to control run off, erosion, and help to slow the water from rains, watering, etc., so that the water can seep into the ground and under the berm, where it creates an underground reservoir of water that your plants can use when they are thirsty.

Swales and berms are artificially built up levies or mounds that stop the flow of water from immediately cascading down a hill, and taking nutrients, topsoil and the precious water with it.

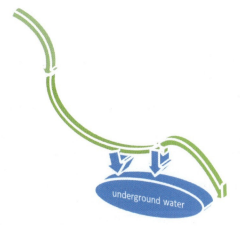

Swales and berms on your terraces will slow downhill water flow so that it can seep into the ground to form pools under the berms.

The nature of permaculture is that your plants are "permanent", since they live in the same spot year after year without replanting. Therefore, these plants have time to grow longer and deeper roots, to reach nutrients and water. Thus, collecting water underground through swales works particularly well for feeding permaculture plants.

Annuals on the other hand don't have time to grow deep roots because in the matter of 3-6 months, annuals must sprout from a seed, grow into a plant, set flowers, create fruit/vegetables, and then ripen that fruit.

The fruit is then carried off and eaten by animals, who excrete, or drop the seeds that will become the new annual plants for next year, where they go through the cycle all over again.

Because of this rapid grow and procreation, annuals don't have time to put down deep roots, so annuals typically need water and nutrients close to the surface.

Perennials, by contrast, stay in one place for many years, and in some instances, don't produce fruit for several years after they first sprout so that they can devote their energy to developing a strong root system, trunk and branches to support that heavy fruit.

This is why the general public often buys established plants for fruit trees and shrubs (like blue berries), so that (as consumers) we don't have to wait as long, to see the "fruits" of our labor. (When you are buying a fruit or nut tree from a nursery, these trees are often already several years old.)

Building a Swale- In Chapter Two, I suggested that you use trees, branches, and other natural material that will decompose over time, as the base of your berms. Once these materials are in place, you can cover these with topsoil and then with mulch, which will give you an area to plant on that will be nutrient rich over time, and that will provide you with not only a way to stop the flow and erosion of water, but also with nutrients that your perennial plants would not otherwise have. Plus-these nutrients are

"free" to you by simply using limbs and trees that you would have otherwise have hauled away or burned in a brush pile.

A word of caution: be certain to bury the dead trees and branches deep enough, and to cover them with enough topsoil and mulch, so that the dead trees that you buried underground will be deeper than the largest and deepest pot of the fruit trees, nut trees and shrubs that you will be planting. In other words, you don't want to be trying to dig through a buried tree, in order to plant the root ball from a new fruit tree deep enough so that it can survive.

In all instances of swales, you will need to be aware of the flow of water relative to each guild, since you want to avoid having your swales all run downhill to one low spot, where you will have a large puddle, or worse yet, overflow into the berm below caused by not having relatively level swales.

This is why it is wise to have your swales follow the contour of your land, so that multiple swales can create semi-circles from one end of the garden to another. If done right, this will allow for even rainwater flow across the entire length of the swale and will avoid certain areas becoming "swampy" while other areas become dry and "desert-like".

The layout your swales with old logs and branches to follow the contour of your permaculture garden.

Fish-scale Swales- If you don't have the contour, slope, or length of space to create berms from one side of your garden to another, you can use smaller swales that trap the water, using a "crescent moon" shape that will help stop run off and create underground water storage for one or more trees and their associated guilds. If your berms are wide enough, you can plant on top of these berms. If not, you can plant your trees within the crescent moon.

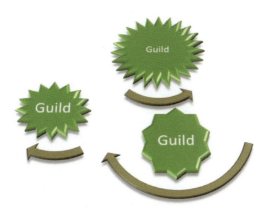

Fish-scale swales can be used to trap water around individual guilds or trees.

Irrigation- Drip hoses, soaker hoses and the like can be connected to pond, cisterns, and pumped water. By laying these hoses on top of berms and laying them in semi-circles around trees and bushes, you can use more efficient drip irrigation to water your most important plants when they are just getting started.

Plan on watering your crops the first season to get them established.

You should also consider a good tripod watering stand (or several of them) in order to get the other plants like herbs and cover crops established, before you have shade and before they have a chance to establish deeper roots. We did this for the first year of our permaculture food forest, and then did not have to use any form of irrigation after that.

Micro-climates- Rocks, bodies of water and other thermal masses (i.e. retaining walls or walls of houses, etc.) create "micro-climates" that can help your more sensitive plants produce fruit sooner and for longer in the season due to the warming effect of these objects.

Microclimates collect heat during the day and give it off at night.

As most people know, rocks or water will absorb heat during the day, and will give off heat at night when the air is cooler. By planting around these microclimates you can reduce the risk of plants getting hit with frost both earlier in the year and later in the year. Thus micro-climates allow you to create a longer growing season for those plants. And ultimately you will be producing more fruit and healthier plants in the long term.

You can take advantage of micro-climates by keeping rocks exposed in various places on your berms. Plants near these "thermal masses" will then be less effected by late spring frosts and early fall frosts as well as generally cold temperatures, because the heat given off at night by these rocks, keeps them warmer, and safer at night, when the sun is gone.

CHAPTER 5
PERMACULTURE GUILDS

For over 1 million years, plants have been growing the way nature intended. And in nature, diverse mixtures of plants generally grow together, and they often have symbiotic relationships, where certain plants directly or indirectly help each other. Thus, these plants do better growing together, than they do growing alone.

It is only in the last 150 years that man, in his wisdom, decided that he could do it better than nature and also make it easier for himself, by planting the same crops together, and in rows (also known as "mono-crops").

Of course rows of mono-crops are not natural; and after years of trying to force mono-crops to work, by using fertilizer and pesticides in both commercial farming and residential gardening, man is starting to realize that maybe Mother Nature knew what was best after all.

If you look at the edge of forest you can see nature and the natural succession of plants in action.

At the edge of a forest you have grasses, weeds and ground covers in the opening, and then as you approach the tall forest tress, there are herbs next, then shrubs like blackberries, then shorter trees that eventually meld into the tall trees of the forest.

Permaculture mimics the edge of a forest, where all the plants in a guild can get water, sunlight, and the protection from winds and cold that each needs.

There are seven layers of a permaculture guild. (1) The tallest layer is the tall tree layer (typically nut trees) 2) the next tallest layer is the short tree layer (typically fruit trees), 3) then the shrub layer (berries), 4) then the herb layer (medicinal and cooking herbs), 5) then the ground cover layer (strawberries, clover, nitrogen fixers, nitrogen accumulators) 6) and then the root crop layer (onions, garlic, potatoes, and other root crops). 7) Lastly you have the vine layer (grapes, passion fruit, peas, pole beans) that naturally grow up your short and tall trees.

By planting in layers, you are essentially planting in 3 dimensions (instead of just planting one dimensional rows on the ground).

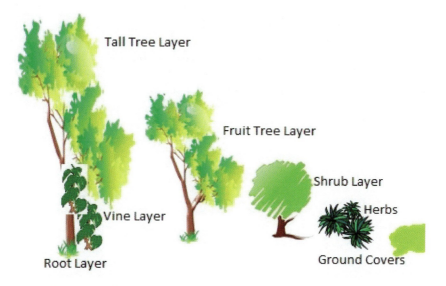

Planting in these 3 dimensions allows you to grow 5x more food per square foot than you can in traditional mono-crop gardening.

As an example, in a 100 sq. ft. space (10' x 10') you can grow a mono-crop like sweet corn, with an average yield of 35 lb. of corn per 100 sq. ft.

However in the same 100 sq. ft. using 3 dimensional permaculture, you can plant an apple tree (with an avg. yield of 51 lb. of fruit), as well as grape vines growing up your apple tree (with an avg. yield of 31 lb.); and strawberries as a ground cover under the tree (with an avg. yield of 102 lb.). So in the same 100 sq. ft., you can grow 184 lb. (51+ 31 + 102= 184) of permaculture fruit in three dimensions, as opposed to a mono-crop planting where you can have 35 lb. of corn (or similar amounts for other typical standard vegetables planted as mono-crops in rows).

184 lbs. of food vs. 35 lbs. of food in the same space. And the 184 lbs. requires far less work on your part. Which sounds like a better deal to you?

Not only does planting in guilds yield more food per square foot, but the companion planting in guilds creates symbiotic relationships that help the plants produce even more food- without fertilizer, and without pesticides.

Fruit Tree Guild- In a typical fruit tree guild you would plant your fruit tree (such as an apple, pear, or peach tree) in the center of the guild.

If you plant onions or garlic around base of tree, mice won't go near it in winter and gird the tree.

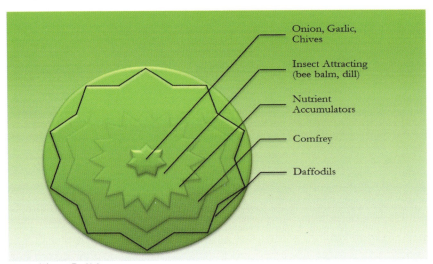

Fruit Tree Guild

If you plant comfrey under the tree, you have a plant that has long leaves, which creates a "green mulch", that shades the soil and keeps moisture from evaporating. Comfrey also has medicinal (wound care- among other things) purposes. Comfrey also can grow a 30' tap root that can reach nutrients and minerals that your other guild plants can't reach. Comfrey brings these nutrients to the surface so that the other plants in the guild can use them. When comfrey leafs die back in the fall, they create a wonderful dried mulch for your other plants.

You can plant various herbs under the tree that can be used for both medicinal and cooking purposes. The little flowers on herbs are insect attractors that bring in pollinating insects, including wasps that are predator insects. These "good bugs" not only pollinate your other crops in the guild, but they also prey on the bad insects that you don't want in your guild.

One of my favorite herbs is Mountain Mint that contains more camphor than any plant I know. It is aromatic, and it is also great for honey bees. The oils on the Mountain Mint, are brought back on the hairs of the bee to the honey bee hive and these oils are shared with other bees in the hive. The oils help the bees to remove mites from their bodies, which makes for healthy bees and more honey production for you.

SECRET GARDEN OF SURVIVAL

If you plant daffodils around the drip line of the tree, or if you plant rosemary in your guilds, it will keep deer away, so they won't be stealing your apples.

You can plant your shrubs (any variety of berry bushes) outside the drip line of the central guild tree, where they can get light and air.

Outside of the shrub layer, you can plant additional herbs including thyme, parsley, sage, oregano, catnip, mint, feverfew (a good headache cure), Echinacea (a great cold remedy), lemon balm (for lemon flavored herbal tea), fennel and dill, to name only a few.

Outside of your herb layer you can plant your ground covers which can be something like strawberries that produce fruit, or something like clover that you can walk on without worry, as you move from guild to guild.

Walnut Guild- Not all guilds are the same. A fruit tree guild may have different plants than a nut tree guild.

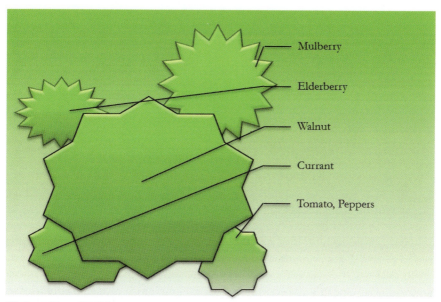

Walnut Tree Guild

For example, did you ever notice a black walnut tree in a neighbor's yard? Did you ever notice what grows underneath the walnut tree?

Well in most cases – nothing grows there. That is because walnut trees don't like competition, so walnuts give off a toxin in their roots.

However, plants in the night shade family (like tomatoes, peppers, etc.), as well as currants, elderberry, hackberry and wolfberry, thrive in this environment. Do some research on your central guild trees, and know what grows with it.

Multiple Guilds- Eventually you will get to a point where you will be planting multiple guilds, so when you start planting your central guild trees, make sure you leave enough room between the trees and the guilds so that the trees don't shade each other out when they grow to full size at maturity.

The biggest problem most people make when planting guilds is not allowing enough room for growth. Remember that not only will your central guild trees grow up and out, but your shrubs and herbs will grow and spread out too.

Another thing to consider is putting buffer plants between different types of guilds. For example, mulberry and Elaeagnus create a transition space that protects neighboring plants form the walnut's root toxins.

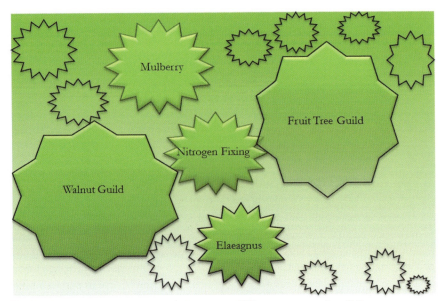

Buffer plants create transitions between different types of guilds.

CHAPTER 6
RAIN WATER COLLECTION

Water is the most important resource for survival for both you and your livestock, not to mention your plants.

Adequate water is particularly important in the early stages of permaculture plant growth, when trees and shrubs are young, and until they have established their deep root systems.

In a grid down situation you most likely will not be able to get water from the utility company, or from a deep well.

And not everyone has a stream, lake, pond, or shallow well on their property. The option of using solar power to pump water up from any well can be extremely expensive.

However, just about everyone, lives under a roof. And many people have multiple roofs on their property (home, shed, garage/carport, barn, etc.). Rain water collection is easy, and the cost of a rainwater collection system per gallon, just about beats anything else you can do. Plus – you won't need electricity to get at your water. And if your rainwater barrels are uphill from your garden, you won't need a pump to get the water to your crops, because you can simply use gravity to water your plants.

Here's how you can calculate rainfall collected per sq. ft. of roof area: 1 sq. ft. of roof area = .623 gallons per inch of rainfall. So as an example- if you had 1000 sq. ft. of roof area, you could collect 623 gallons of water for every inch of rain that fell on your roof. Here is a simple formula:

__ sq. ft. roof surface x .623 x __ inches of rainfall = gallons collected

Typical Rain Water Collection System- A rain water catchment system can be as simple as having a water tight barrel under an existing downspout from your roof. Having a spigot on the bottom of the barrel allows you to attach a simple garden hose to the barrel and use that to water your plants.

A downspout diverter allows you to flush the majority of debris from your roof, before the water goes into your rain barrel.

A **first flush downspout diverter** is a simple way to filter out the majority of leaves, pine needles, bugs and bird droppings that may be on your roof, and washed off by the rain. Instead of these materials going directly into your rain collection barrel, they first go into this pipe, and then once the pipe is full, the rest of the (cleaner) water goes into the barrel. Then, after the rain is over, you can flush this diverter of its roof debris by simply opening a valve or "clean-out" in the diverter.

If you use HDPE (High Density Poly Ethylene) (food grade plastic) tanks, you can use these tanks to collect rainwater for your family and your livestock to drink from, as well as for your plants. Since this type of plastic does not leach petro chemicals into the water, these barrels are safe to drink from, as long as you do not have bacteria in the water. (Before drinking the water directly from the tank, you may want to consider boiling the water or a filtration system that removes biological contaminants.)

Also if your tank is colored so that it does not allow light through, then algae won't grow in the water either.

A rain water collection system can be used for watering plants, feeding livestock, or for use in your home in an emergency.

Below Ground Rain Water System- You can use a larger tank that will hold more water if you put a cistern underground. You can use a screen to filter out debris at the top of the entrance to the tank.

You can retrieve the water from the tank by either a hand pump in the tank, or you can have a pipe coming underground from the bottom of the tank that is connected to a spigot, attached to hoses to water the garden.

You can use a larger underground tank to catch rainwatet as well.

CHAPTER 7
VEGETABLE AND HERB GARDEN

Although I advocate inter-planting your annuals with your perennials throughout your survival garden (to take advantage of all the good things you have going on in terms of insect attracting bugs, etc.), inter-planting among your perennials can make things like root crops (sweet potatoes, potatoes, carrots, onions, etc.) hard to find at the end of the season once the plant tops have died back…

Here is an option (that at least is not traditional "row planting") for growing your annuals/vegetables outside your perennial food forest, and for other crops that you will want to protect, such as seedlings, tender young plants, etc., until they get established.

A **keyhole garden** – is so called because the shape of the garden looks like an old fashioned keyhole.

One benefit of keyhole gardens is that they use less path space than planting in straight rows and they also uses less space than raised beds.

That is because most gardens planted in single rows need as much space for paths between the rows as the row plants take up themselves. For example, to plant 50 square feet of crops in straight rows, you need an additional 50 square feet of path. Thus, you need 100 sq. ft. of available area to plant only 50 sq. ft. of crops.

Raised beds by contrast, need 10 sq. ft. of path for every 50 sq. ft. of plants.

But a keyhole bed only needs 6 sq. ft. of path, because the garden literally wraps around the path. Thus, in a keyhole garden, you have less wasted space used by paths, and less ground that ends up getting compacted from continually walking on it. So if you are trying to maximize your food production in the space you have, keyhole gardens can provide a solution.

A keyhole garden saves path space when planting herbs and annuals.

A keyhole garden is often planted in zone 1, close to the house/kitchen, so that you can get at these vegetables without having to walk or search for them.

Like the rest of your permaculture garden, you will still want to surround your keyhole garden with herbs, and insect attracting plants, that will help protect it from the bad bugs.

Furthermore, planting taller crops around the edges will help disguise this garden so it is not an obvious garden to passersby. After all the work you will have done to create your disguised permaculture survival garden, you don't want to let others know you have a garden there, by planting visible vegetables.

Companion planting is also a key aspect of keyhole gardening, since you can interplant different types of annuals that work better together than they would by themselves.

For example, a symbiotic relationship exists between tomatoes with asparagus, basil, carrots, chive, garlic, onions, and parsley. Whereas you might have another keyhole garden planted with cucumbers, beans, cabbage, corn, peas, and radishes.

Also based on the depth and the width of plants and their root systems, plants onions, lettuce, and carrots work together because the neither shades the other out, and neither root systems compete.

If you use keyhole gardening, make sure that you rotate your plants each year (don't plant the same things in the same space year after year) or certain nutrients will be depleted. And worse yet, bad bugs that like a certain plant will have dropped eggs that will attack next year's plants if you plant the same ones in the same place.

You can also plant ground cover/ nitrogen fixing crops like clover, buckwheat, and alfalfa, etc. (see Chapter 9) in the off season to help bring back the nutrients to these areas of high intensity annual nutrient consumption.

CHAPTER 8
INFRASTRUCTURE FOR THE GARDEN

Spend some time observing your land before you DO anything.

Observe-Before you do anything; spend some time walking your land after it has been cleared. Walk it during sunny days and notice the sunny areas, hot spots, shady areas, cold spots, how the wind moves across the land and how long the sun is in any particular place throughout the day. Visit the property during and after rain storms, watch were rain flows, where there are spots of erosion. These observations will give you a good basis on which to build your plan.

Determine the elements of your guilds- Make a plan to only purchase plants that will actually grow in your geographic area. There is no sense trying to plant citrus trees outdoors in New England. By the same token, certain types of blueberries and certain types of apple trees grow well in New England, but don't do well in the south.

However, there are species of blueberries and apple tress that will grow well in the south, so do a little research on the internet. Or stop by a reputable nursery, where you can talk to people that really know something about plants that will thrive in your area.

Figure out what kind of plants you want to grow and start making a list. Study their various attributes- how much sun, how much water, and chill hours that they require and then start to put together a list of where these plants should go in your survival garden master plan.

Native Varieties of Plants- Often when you buy plants from the big box stores, these plants are part of a master sales plan for these big box stores, and the plants you get are not native to your area and they may not do well in your area.

In addition, these plants where grown somewhere else and have most likely been shipped from across the country. Before they left these plants were pumped full of drugs to make them look good while they are sitting in your local store. But just like what happens to a drug addict when the drugs wear off, your plants can wither and die within months of getting them home.

So wherever possible, try to grow native plants- plants that are indigenous to your area. It is even better if they were originally propagated and grown in pots where you live.

If you can find a nursery that has indigenous plants that were propagated locally, the plants will be more adapted to the extremes of heat and cold in your environment, as well as your rainfall, your local plant diseases, etc.

And if you can find a local nursery that propagates local varieties of fruit trees, shrubs and herbs, that also understands permaculture, then you have hit the jackpot! It is worth doing some research to find one. There is nothing worse than spending the time to plant a guild and have parts of it die, because the plants just weren't native to the area and could not handle the environment.

Start with a Plan- Now that you know what grows in your area, and what plants you can use based on your landscape and climate, it is time to decide where to place your specific guild trees based on your earlier observations of dry, wet, sunny, and shady areas in your garden.

You also need to consider the "zones" within your garden. Think of zones to be like concentric circles emanating from your house in zone 1. Zone 1 should be closest you your house and/or at the top of the hill on your property and zone 1 should contain the trees, shrubs and herbs that will be in most need of attention, or that may need the most protection to get started (like keeping deer away from them at night).

Layout your garden by zones, with Zone 1 being the closest.

Zone 2 will be just outside of zone 1, and zone 3 will be outside of zone 2. Ultimately the guilds that you plant furthest away, will need the least attention and protection, and will be in the "wildest" and most natural areas.

Having wilder areas that are further away from your house, also gives you the opportunity to start your permaculture a little at a time, so that you don't have to plant everything at once. The wild areas will then have a chance to develop and pioneer plants (weeds) can move in that will help develop the soil to make it more fertile, and more acceptable for your future guilds.

Likewise you can plant crops like buckwheat and clover in these further zones, to help develop the soil, prevent erosion, and prepare for future guilds.

Draw up your plan using graph paper and a pencil (with a big eraser!) because you will probably be making a lot of changes, revisions, etc. as you go through this process. Keep in mind that it doesn't have to be "pretty"- it just needs to be accurate.

SECRET GARDEN OF SURVIVAL

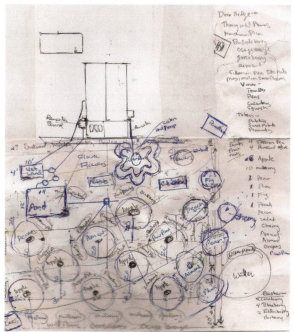

Start with a plan and lay it out

Start with laying out the main tree (fruit or nut) of each guild, allowing at least 20' in diameter to keep typical mature fruit trees from touching each other and shading out other guild plants.

Once you have your trees in place on the plan, fill in with shrubs, herbs and ground covers. Make sure to allow for those secondary plants to have access to the sun. (In other words, don't plan on putting blueberry bushes directly behind your fruit trees...you want to off-set them a bit to give them sunlight.) Think in 3 dimensions when working out your plan, and make sure that your herb layer is not blocked from the sun by your shrub layer, as well. Once you have it on paper, then you can start working out your plan on the land.

Layout your berms and terraces using the not-so-perfect logs that you saved from clearing the forest. Lay them end to end in somewhat parallel rows to mark your future berms. Once you do this, you will get a good indication of how wide or tight your terraces and berms will be, and what grade/ steepness the downhill side of your berms will be.

Stake out your guilds along your future swales and berms.

Stake out the guilds- Guild spacing should be based on the main tree (fruit or nut) that will be at the center of each of your guilds. Allow at least 20' in diameter to keep typical mature fruit trees from touching each other and shading out other guild plants. Place stakes with tape flags in the ground where you think each of these trees ought to be, based on your plan. It is best to get yourself a long (50' or more) tape measure, and to do this with more than one person. Don't forget to measure from every direction to determine if any of the stakes are less that 20' from any of the others. You may have to measure these stakes, and move them a number of times before you get it right.

Invest in Equipment- When we built our terraces, we hired a local backhoe operator at $30/hr. to do the major earth moving and to form the terraces. In about 10 hours of time, he did everything that we needed to have done on half an acre. I couldn't have moved the huge rocks by hand, and even if we could have done it by hand, it would have taken years to do the ground work without the backhoe. Do yourself a favor. Do the big job with big equipment while you can, and it will give you a lot more time to get the other work done that you will need to do by hand to make your Secret Garden of Survival a working reality.

Hiring a good equipment operator is a very small investment that can save you time in getting your Secret Garden of Survival established.

Share the Plan- Make sure the people that are helping you understand what you want to do, so they can help to make sure your plan is carried out. Do it right the first time.

Terraces- The most important aspect of your Secret Garden of Survival's infrastructure will be the terraces/berms/swales on which you build the rest of your garden. Think of them as the foundation on which you will build the rest of your house.

To get started, before you cut too deeply into the side of the hill, have your backhoe operator scrape the topsoil off your south side slope, and dump the top soil in piles at the end of where each terrace will be.

After removing the topsoil layer, cut into the side of the hill with the backhoe to remove the under-layer of clay and gravel, in order to make your terraces based on the layout of your logs. Cover the logs with the dirt you are removing to form the flat terrace area, and place the excess dirt on the downhill side of each terrace. The covered logs will decompose under the dirt and will give you natural fertilizer for the trees and shrubs you will plant later on those berms.

The size (width and height) of the terraces will depend on the steepness of your property's original slope and the number of berms you have set up. For example, on our half an acre, we had seven terraces that were 150' in length. The flat parts of the terraces are 10-20 feet wide in places, and there is an average of 6' differential in height between one terrace and the next one above it. That has given us more than enough space to plant plenty of guilds.

As your heavy equipment is putting dirt over the downhill side of your terraces, you can leave some of the big rocks that fall out of the bucket in place to create micro climates for future plantings. For the most part you can also leave many of the dead roots and tree parts in place, as they will add nutrients to your soil as they decompose over time.

Once the terraces are cut into the hill, put the topsoil that you saved back in place on top of each berm and over the downhill edge of each terrace. This way you can re-use as much good topsoil as possible and that will give you a better start when it comes to planting your guilds.

Once you cover your berms and the downhill sides of your terraces, you probably won't have enough top soil left over to cover the flat surface area of the terraces. So you will most likely have exposed clay and/or gravel on these flat surfaces. You can either bring in more topsoil or decomposed mulch to cover the flat areas.

Once you are finished with the terraces, you should be well on your way to starting your Secret Garden of Survival.

And, as it turns out, you will now have even more surface area available to plant than you would if you had left the land with its original downhill slope. This is actually a matter of simple geometry. A side view of a terrace is much like looking at the side of a triangle. In geometry the sum of the two shorter legs of any triangle are always greater than the length of the hypotenuse (the longer side). So the "legs" that you have cut into the hill will actually give you more planting area, than the slope of the hill would have given you if you had not cut into the hill. (See triangle illustration below.)

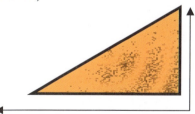

Terraces give you more surface area to plant on than the original slope.

So aside from water retention and erosion prevention, creating berms, swales and terraces gives you the additional benefit of planting more in less space.

Additionally, you can use the downhill sides of the terraces for planting ground covers, herbs, and for annual vining plants like squash, cucumber, pumpkin, watermelon, and cantaloupe. By planting annual vining plants near the top of the berm and letting them run downhill, their vines won't interfere with the growth of other plants and this will give you more space to plant other non-vining plants, elsewhere in your garden.

Grey Water Wetland- If you are going to put in a grey water wetland and a retention/duck pond as part of your Secret Garden of Survival, the ideal time to do the ground work is when you are creating the terraces. Since you will already have the heavy equipment on site, digging two holes and a couple of trenches will be less costly than doing it later. Furthermore, by doing it now, you will have less potential negative impact on your garden, than bringing in heavy equipment later, once you have started planting your guilds.

Your wetland should hold about 600 gallons of water, so the hole needs to be about 4 ft. wide x 10 ft. long and 4 ft. deep. Clear any sharp rocks and roots from the sides of the hole with a hand shovel. Smooth the sides of the hole and make the shape uniform enough so that you can fold over a pond liner into the hole.

Unfinished wetland using a pool liner, crushed stone and metal baffles.

You will also need a trench to run a 2" drain pipe from your house to the wetland, buried below the frost line. (You can use the backhoe for this effort as well.) Of course the pipe will need to slope downhill from the house to the wetland at ¼" per foot, so that the water will flow into the wetland and not back into your house. So dig the trench accordingly.

How you connect your interior grey water source onto the exterior pipe coming up to your house from the wetland will be up to you. You may want to enlist the help of a licensed plumber to help you do so.

The wetland end of the 2" pipe should empty into the bottom of the wetland at the end furthest away from outlet. (The "outlet" is the end of your grey water wetland that will drain into the pond that will be downstream of your grey water wetland.)

You can purchase a standard pond liner for your wetland or you can use an exterior vinyl pool liner, as long as it is turned inside out. Turning it inside out will make sure that the chemical UV treatment (on what would have been the "sunny side"- the side with the decorative lining) will not leach into your pond water. This will keep these chemicals from polluting your water – water which may be used by fish, ducks and your plants in the future.

2" grey water pipe from house connected to a diffuser in wetland basin.

Once you have the pond liner in place in the hole, spread it out over the embankment (you will be covering this with dirt and mulch later) and begin filling the liner floor with crushed stones (the type you would normally use in a drain field). You will then have to cut a hole in the pond liner in order to punch your 2" pipe through into the wetland. You will also have to use pool fittings (for vinyl pool) to seal the hole around the 2" pipe.

Use the best silicone that you can buy in order to seal around both sides of the pipe where it goes through the vinyl. Connect the pipe to a diffuser so that the water will have a chance to seep down into the crushed stones without clogging up the pipe end with sediment.

Begin filling the pond with more crushed stone. Put the bigger stones closer to the 2" pipe inlet and diffuser (to filter out bigger particles first), with smaller stones closer to the wetland outlet.

Between the inlet and the outlet, you will want to place baffles (which can be as simple as standing metal roofing sheets on end). The objective of the baffles is to slow the water flow. So place the baffles in such a way as to have the water go over one baffle and then under the next one.

You can place baffles the width of your wetland, at about 2-3' apart, and perpendicular to the water flow toward the outlet (see photo of the unfinished wetland above). Finish filling the wetland with stone until you can no longer see the baffles. Then cover the liner on the sides with clay, dirt, and lastly with mulch, so you can plant cover crops on the edges.

Later (once you have water flowing into the wetland) you can place aquatic plants directly into the crushed stones of your wetland, including cattails, bulrushes and other edible plants that will feed off the grey water wastes and help to clean the water.

The outlet of the wetland then simply over flows into the trickle ponds below it. (Hint- build up the sides of the wetland so that they are higher than the outlet end, so that the water has to flow by gravity into trickle ponds).

Finished grey water wetland with overflow into future trickle ponds.

Stream and trickle ponds- Use pieces of the pond liner that you may have left over from trimming the liner used with the grey water system for use in your stream and trickle ponds. Line the vinyl pieces with rocks and gravel along the sides to cover the liner from sun exposure. The rocks and gravel will also slow the water flow and help with aeration of the water before the water enters your pond. (It will look more like a natural stream once plants are established and water begins flowing.)

Stream and trickle ponds flow from wetland into larger pond.

Retention & Duck Pond- While you still have the backhoe, dig a hole for your pond adjacent to your wetland and trickle ponds so that the pond is downhill from both (for gravity flow of water from the grey water wetland). Make the hole approximately 14 ft. in diameter and 6 ft. deep in the center. Do the major work with a back-hoe, and save the rocks you pull out of the hole for later.

Once the major hole is has been dug out, you will have to do the rest of the work by a hand shovel. Make the sides smooth and remove any sharp rocks that could puncture your vinyl pond liner. The hole itself doesn't need to be perfectly round. It is actually better and more natural if it is not. Remember that this will be home to your fish, your ducks and what they will eat, so little indentions and "coves" for tiny fish to hide in, is not a bad thing.

Most likely you will have tree roots that will be protruding into the hole that the backhoe made. You will want to cut all roots back to the wall, and pull out whatever ones you can.

You will want to install a 2 inch diameter drain pipe coming out of the bottom third of the pond. This is so that you can keep the pond from overflowing and so that you can use the pond water (which will be rich in nutrients) on your crops when you need to.

Put a screen on the pond end of the 2 inch pipe to keep small fish from being sucked through it when you open the valve down below.

Junction box to connect hoses for distributing pond water to the garden.

Put the 2 inch pipe through the vinyl lining much like you did for the grey water wetland. Dig a trench downhill to a junction box where you can connect the 2 inch pipe to a 2 inch ball valve and then neck down the pipe coming out of the valve outlet, onto a ¾ inch ball valve. From there you can connect one or more spigots that you can then attach to garden hoses.

It would be wise to back fill this trench with gravel and crushed stone using the same kind of crushed stone that you used in your grey water wetland. Then you can make this the lowest edge of your pond, so that the pond has a place to overflow safely and overflow water can drain into the ground, instead of over your embankments.

Line your pond walls with old carpet to keep roots and small rocks from poking through the liner.

To keep roots from pushing through the vinyl liner; line the pond walls with old wall to wall carpet from the dump. Then spread the pool liner inside out and place the liner into place on top of the carpet, being careful not to rip the liner while you are working with it inside the hole.

Leave enough liner on the top of the pool embankment area to hold the liner in place with rocks. Put gravel and a few large rocks in the bottom of the pond so that the fish will have a rock grotto that they can hide in.

Spread the liner over the embankments, place a drain near the bottom of the pond, and create a low point on the embankment so overflow will only go where you want it to.

Cover the outside perimeter with dirt, rocks and mulch deep enough to allow plants to take root. Make sure that all sides of the pond are higher than the outlet/overflow side to allow for overflow that won't cause erosion. You don't want to have a "levy break" that causes a downhill flood in your garden when the pond is full from rainwater and grey water flow.

Next, fill the pond with water. You can use water from your cisterns/rain water collection, etc. and fill the rest with rainfall after that. You will want to monitor the water level closely to insure that the when the pond gets close to being full, that it overflows into your special overflow area, and does not go over the embankments. If it is close, then add more clay, dirt and mulch to the embankments. Then seed the embankments with fast germinating buckwheat to hold the soil in place.

Grey water system to the right flows into stream and trickle ponds in the center and finally flows into finished pond below.

CHAPTER 9
PREPARING THE GROUND

No one wants to worry about their dirt. After all, it's just dirt- right? ...Wrong!

Your dirt contains all the food that your plants will eat. And if your plants eat well, they will grow well. And if your plants grow well, they will produce good food, so you will eat well too!

Creating good soil is important, especially if you are starting from red clay. In fact, almost nothing grows in red clay. And if you don't cover the red clay with good soil or mulch, and the clay is left to bake in the sun, your landscape will turn into one solid brick.

Soil is the support system for all plants; it provides a balanced diet of nutrients that allow those plants to grow. And believe it or not soil is not just inanimate sand and minerals thrown together. Good soil is quite alive.

Soil organisms live in the soil. They include molds and bacteria that breakdown organic matter that is then eaten by mold mites, beetles, protozoa, roundworms (nematodes), sowbugs, roundworms, earthworms, millipedes, snails and slugs. Those organisms are then consumed by mites, centipedes, ground beetles and ants, which leave their droppings that then, become nutrients that your plants can consume.

Soil life recycles organic matter that the plants use for food. Some of those organisms also break down the minerals into nutrients that the plants can use. Without this soil life, the plants could not feed themselves and they would die.

This is another case against using pesticides. That is because all too often, when using pesticides, they end up in the soil. And not only do pesticides kill bad bugs you are trying to eliminate, they also can kill the micro-organisms in the soil that are critical to the breakdown and release of nutrients for the plants to use. In short- if you kill your soil, you kill your plants.

Good (Decomposed) Mulch- You are going to need some really good mulch. I'm not talking about the kind of mulch that has been dried, died and fried to look pretty. I'm talking about the kind of mulch that looks like brown dirt, that is warm to the touch, and that has steam rising out of it when you put a shovel into it. I'm talking about the kind of mulch that has an earthy, organic, rich smell to it. I'm talking about mulch that is breaking down, and that is full of microorganisms that are doing the job.

Good, decomposed mulch is an essential asset to your garden for several reasons.

Put good decomposed mulch on your berms to bring back life to your soil.

First, mulch stops erosion. When it rains, rainwater seeps into the ground through the mulch, instead of running down your property in rivers and taking all your soil's rich nutrients with it.

Mulch stops water evaporation. Mulch keeps water vapor from leaving the soil when the sun is beating down on it. And if your ground experiences too much evaporation, it becomes hard. Then important soil organisms die, and water is unavailable for sensitive roots.

Mulch adds organic material and organisms to the soil. Decomposed mulch adds living organisms, and nutrients to the soil, that your plants would not otherwise have available, especially if you have just stripped your ground bare, to make your swales.

One very important note on acquiring mulch: When you are shopping for a truck-load (or two) of mulch, make sure that the mulch is herbicide free! Be wary of "free mulch" that you can get from the city or county public works department. Often times this mulch comes from roadside debris that was bush-hogged and then wood chipped from road ways. Aside from this mulch containing potential roadside salts, petrochemicals (oil, gasoline), etc., often these road crews have sprayed herbicide on the plants prior to their removal and wood-chipping for mulch. Some of these herbicides (Round-up, etc.) can keep plants from growing for years. And once they leach into your soil from contaminated mulch, you may never be able to get rid of them.

Mycelium- Ever scratch the surface of good topsoil and see what looks like tiny white roots running through it?

Mycelium is like roots running through your soil that connects everything in your garden.

That is Mycelium- it's the vegetative part of a fungus, consisting of a mass of branching, thread-like roots. When two compatible mycelia join together, that resulting mycelium may form fruiting bodies such as mushrooms, puffballs, toadstools, and truffles.

Mycelia are vital in their role of the decomposition of plant material. They contribute to the organic matter of soil, and their growth releases carbon dioxide back into the atmosphere. (Plants consume carbon dioxide, and give us back oxygen.) Some mycelium increases the efficiency of water and nutrient absorption of plants, as well as their resistance to some plant diseases. Mycelia are also an important food source for many soil invertebrates.

When two compatible mycelia join together, that resulting mycelium may form fruiting bodies such as mushrooms, puffballs, toadstools, and truffles.

The largest single organism in the world may have been a 2,400-acre site in eastern Oregon that had a contiguous growth of mycelium running through it, before logging roads had been cut across it. This single organism was estimated to be the size of 1,665 football fields and was 2,200 years old.

Mycelium is like having a communications network running through your garden. Some research even suggests that messages can be sent from one area to another in a garden, calling for nutrients to be sent to areas that may need them in other areas of the garden.

That's why I like to say that you can think Mycelium as being like the "Force" in *Star Wars*…"it is the force that binds everything together".

Preparing the Ground (by planting "fertilizing" plants)

Nitrogen Fixers and Nutrient Accumulators- These plants put nutrients into the soil. Nitrogen fixers take nitrogen out of the atmosphere and make it available to the other plants around them. (Nitrogen is a key ingredient in fertilizers.) Nutrient accumulators gather nutrients that other plants can't reach or synthesize and makes these nutrients available to the other plants around them.

Clover- Clover is a commonly misunderstood plant and often thought of as a weed, primarily by people who are trying to grow "nice lawns". The truth is that clover grows because the soil is deficient in nitrogen. Clover is good for surrounding plants, and good for bees. When you look for clover seeds, make sure that you get a clover that is a perennial (not an annual- like Crimson Clover) and make sure the type you plant will grow in your area. (I wasted a lot of time and money trying to grow expensive New Zealand and White Dutch clovers- only to find that it wouldn't take in my area.)

Buckwheat - Buckwheat germinates in three days and is one of my all-time favorite nitrogen fixers (although it is an annual and will most likely have to be replanted each year that you use it).

Buckwheat is a great first plant to use in a brand new, cleared garden. It takes hold quickly, and it sets down roots to hold the soil in place. Its seeds are "pyramid-shaped" and they have the wonderful property of sticking where you throw them on bare soil. Unlike round seeds that tend to roll down-hill on the sides of berms, buckwheat stays where you put it. So it is a great starter crop, especially for the sides of your terraces to prevent erosion.

Buckwheat seeds are pyramid shaped, so they don't roll down hills.

Plus you can eat the "fruit". (Buckwheat seeds are not officially a grain- they are a fruit.) You can thresh buckwheat like you would wheat, collect the seeds, and then grind them up to use instead of, or in combination with, other types of flour to make healthy and tasty dishes (i.e. buckwheat pancakes).

Buckwheat germinates in only 3 days, holds the soil in place, puts nitrogen in the soil, flowers constantly, and attracts good bugs to your garden.

Buckwheat flowers constantly and can grow to 4 ft. tall. It is a great attractor of bees and other predator/pollinators. Thus, buckwheat is great to plant among your new perennial plants, so that they can have an insect army to defend them against the "bad bugs".

If you start early in the spring, you may get as many as three different crops of buckwheat during the course of one season. (As the buckwheat matures, it then drops its seeds, which then will sprout news plants in the same place.)

Peas and Beans (and other Legumes) - Our familiar peas and beans not only create food for us, but they also fix nitrogen. They are therefore great to plant around your newly planted bushes and trees.

If you wrap fencing around your trees and shrubs like I did (to protect them from deer, and rodents) you can plant peas and beans around the base of your fencing so that the trees and bushes get the benefit of the nitrogen fixing, and so that the peas and beans have a ready-made trellis to grow on. (It makes them easy for you to pick too.)

Peanuts- Peanuts are another legume that fixes nitrogen. Peanuts grow more like bush beans, in that they do not climb or crawl. At the end of the season you simply loosen the soil around the stem after the leaves start to turn yellow, and gently pull up the plant- which will have roots full of white peanuts. Let them dry by hanging them (stems and all) out in the sun a few days, and they will turn the familiar brown and will be ready to eat, or to be processed for things like peanut butter and peanut cooking oil.

Peanuts fix nitrogen, and can provide you with healthy food.

Mustard- The tiny mustard seed can eventually create a huge plant. Mustard is another nitrogen fixer. Mustard plants can be eaten like lettuce when they are young and are great on sandwiches. It's like eating spicy lettuce. The mustard plants will eventually "bolt" (grow tall) to produce seed pods with mustard seeds. You can collect the pods and remove the seeds for planting next year, or you can grind up the seeds and mix with vinegar, to make the condiment we know as mustard.

The mustard plant is also a great "trap plant" for pest bugs. For example, Harlequin bugs will prefer to be on mustard, and will mate there, before they consume other plants in your garden. So you can catch them in the act and squish them by hand to get rid of them, before they eat your other plants.

Mustard grows from a tiny seed to a big plant that can provide leaves for salads, seeds for condiments, and can act as a trap plant for bad bugs.

Dandelion- There is a reason you see this "weed" in open spaces, and in lawns. Nature abhors a vacuum. And since the dandelion is a pioneer plant, it will grow when nothing else will. Dandelion helps to fix the soil, so other plants can move in and succeed it. If they are in your lawn, it is because you have deficiencies in the soil- probably caused by fertilizers and insecticides. They are a great plant to have in your garden- and they are edible too.

Vetch- Vetch is another natural "weed" that crawls along the ground. It often spreads in circles, while it fixes nitrogen for other plants.

Alfalfa- Alfalfa has a tap root that can go down 30 ft. into the ground and pull up nutrients and minerals deep in the soil that other plants (including your fruit trees) cannot reach. Once these plants die back for the season, these plants leach their nutrients back into the soil so that these minerals can be used by the other plants. Alfalfa is another example of how a "pioneer plant" paves the way for other plants to thrive in the future.

Alfalfa is also a staple crop for livestock. It creates a highly protein rich hay, that can be used to feed your cattle, goats, rabbits and other animals that create protein for you.

Strawberries should be planted as a ground cover. Strawberries will help set down roots that hold the soil in place, and they create a type of "green mulch" while growing across the ground. Once strawberries bear their first fruit, they spread with vining type shoots that anchor into the ground and create more strawberry plants. Of course strawberries also provide you with delicious edible fruit. If you purchase an "ever-bearing" variety, you will have a main crop of strawberries early in the spring, and then multiple crops, yielding fruit all the time throughout the summer.

Plants for the livestock: (and grains for you). Aside from alfalfa that we mention, you may want to consider plants like oats, wheat, and rye to plant in your open areas that are further away from your main crops (in zones 3, 4 or 5). These plants are grasses that can produce hay, straw and seeds for your livestock and for you.

Oats, wheat and rye can be used as grains that you can store and eat, that your livestock can eat, and that can be milled into flour for baking, etc. You can also ferment these grains to make beverages, and alcohol for cleaning, fuel, and medicine.

Honey Bees-Perhaps I should have included honey bees in the garden infrastructure chapter, but it made no sense installing bees in your garden, if you don't have anything for them to eat.

So once you have your nitrogen fixers and buckwheat growing, think about adding a vital workforce to your garden- honey bees.

Honey bees and other pollinators have a symbiotic relationship with you.

To produce fruit, nuts and vegetables, plants need to be pollinated. Without pollination, there will be no food for you.

A permaculture survival garden is a great haven for bees. Since there is no use of pesticides or fertilizers that can harm them, you are providing the bees with safe, non-toxic food for their colonies.

In nature, bees will travel as far as 5 miles to seek out nectar and pollen. As a beekeeper, you don't know what your bees could get into in that 5 mile radius. One of your neighbors may have sprayed Seven Dust on their flowers and crops thinking they would keep the off bad bugs. Unfortunately, pesticides are indiscriminate poisons and the good bugs get killed too. Bees often bring these poisons back to the hive and these poisons can kill an entire hive. (Pesticides are one potential cause of Colony Collapse Disorder.)

With a permaculture survival garden, the bees don't have to travel far, because you are providing a constant source of flowers that are blooming at all different times throughout the year. Therefore, your bees don't have to collect their food outside of your property. This also means that the bees spend less time travelling, so worker bees can make more trips per day bringing food back to their hives. Aside from pollinating your crops, bees of course manufacture honey. Thus, more honey can be created from those same bees each year.

Honey has been called nature's perfect food.

Honey kills bacteria, viruses, and fungus. In fact, if bottled and capped so that humidity cannot get in, nothing will grow in honey so it will not spoil.

Honey is nature's perfect food.

Honey is a great storage food. In fact, honey lasts practically forever. Archeologists have found honey in Egyptian tombs that was 3000 years old and still edible!

We have been using honey since the dawn of man. Cave paintings depict images of people gathering honey as long as 12,000 years ago.

Honey contains a tremendous number of enzymes, which have medicinal and anti-allergenic properties.

Honey is a great energy food. And honey can be used for cooking as a substitute for sugar. After your stores of sugar run out after a grid down situation, you may not be able to get sugar again. So honey would be a valuable replacement.

Honey can be used to make alcohol. Mead (honey wine) was the first fermented beverage of man. Mead was valuable for travel because unlike water that got rancid after a short time, man could take mead with him on journeys to drink. And aside from drinking mead, you can distill the alcohol from the wine to store food, clean, disinfect, etc.

Honey is a great internal medicine. It kills germs that could be killing you. That old saying about "a spoonful of honey" has a lot of truth to it.

Honey is also a great external medicine. If you put honey on wounds, they won't get infected. If you have an infection, honey will kill the infection so the wound can heal. Honey has been used in some of the worst cases of infection, where patients have necrosis from diabetes. These patients literally had toes falling off. When other conventional medicines failed, honey stopped the infection and allowed these people to heal.

You can also make candles, lip balm, and lubricants, from bees wax.

You can collect 60 lbs. of honey per hive per year.

If you manage your bees properly, you can collect 60lbs of honey per year per hive. That can go a long way toward creating food, medicine, and cleaning products in a survival situation.

Even if you don't want to tend to the bees yourself, your local bee keepers association often has individuals with hives who are looking for a good place to collect pollen and nectar for their bees so that they can collect the honey.

The bee keeper will do all the work. All you have to do is provide some undisturbed space for a bee yard on the west side of your property. (You want the entrance of the hive to face toward the morning sun- so they will wake up and get active earlier- and do more pollinating, and make more honey.)

The bee keeper will love it, and you can even negotiate a deal to get part of the honey that he collects, for allowing him space on your property.

CHAPTER 10
PLANTING YOUR FOOD FOREST

Equipment- You are going to need some basic equipment to get started planting your Survival Garden, so the first thing you will need to do is get yourself three good shovels.

Essential equipment for planting your Secret Garden of Survival.

You need a long handle spade (a curved back and pointed shovel) for deep digging and heavy lifting without hurting your back. Make sure the handle is smooth, so it is easy on your hands. (You will be using the shovel a lot, so there is no sense getting blisters that will slow you down.)

You will also need a short handle spade. But this one should have a chopping edge on the side to use for clearing brush, as well as a pointed but serrated blade on the tip of the shovel for cutting through gravel, hard clay, roots, and yes, even for cutting through some softer rocks.

You will also need a long handle flat blade shovel, for spreading mulch and shaking it out slowly.

You should find a 2 wheeled wheel barrow. This works so much better than a wheel barrow with only one wheel. It holds more stuff and is far more stable, which will be important when you are trying to transport your plants and your mulch down hills and around your terraces.

I have found a little green wagon with a dump function an invaluable piece of equipment. Even though it has a smaller bed and holds less than the wheelbarrow, this little cart is easier to handle, and move around the berms. I dare say that I moved about 150 yards of mulch with this little cart- and that's a lot of mulch!

Good gloves are a must. To avoid blisters when using shovels, to keep dirt out of your hands when digging, to keep your hands safe, and to keep from getting pricked by thorny plants, you deserve to get yourself a great pair (or two) of gloves. I find that gloves with leather palms and fingers, that have breathable, stretchable fabric around the wrist and on the back of the hand, work well.

Good gloves, good boots and knee pads are a must for planting.

Since you will be spending a good deal of time on the ground getting close and personal to your plants, having a good pair of knee pads is really helpful. It will save your knees, as well as the knees of your pants!

Another important item is a good set of boots. You will be stepping on a lot of stuff that could go right through sneakers or thin soled shoes. Plus high top boots keep dirt and critters out of your socks. I find that the new US Army issue combat boot is one of the best to use in the garden. Millions of dollars of our tax money was used to develop boots and clothing for our military that was durable, comfortable, breathable, water resistant, and that would protect feet from the worst terrain.

How to plant- Well, you are now ready to start planting. But before you start digging a hole, get yourself a large piece of cardboard that you can pile your dirt on.

Dig hole 2-3 x the diameter of pot; put the dirt on a large piece of cardboard.

When digging, you may go through good top soil, gravel, or any combination of rocks, roots and hard clay. If you put the dirt on a large piece of cardboard, you can separate rocks and clay from your good dirt. Also you won't mess up the good mulch that you already put down on your berms. And, it is far easier to dump dirt back around the hole or in your wheelbarrow by simply picking up the cardboard and using it as a funnel.

Dig your hole so that it is 2-3 times the size of the diameter of the plant's container pot, and make the hole a good 6" deeper than the container to allow room for the root ball to grow. Mix equal parts of decomposed mulch with the best dirt from the hole in a wheelbarrow. Put some of this mixture of mulch and dirt back into the hole and then soak the mixture in the hole with a combination of water and hormone mix added. (I use a product called Superthrive. It contains 50 vitamins and plant hormones, to make roots take up carbon-hydrogen-oxygen groups that result in stimulating root growth for newly established plants.) It only takes a tiny capful of this stuff mixed in with a big bucket of water. You don't need to use much.

A good vitamin and hormone mix helps stimulates your plants' roots to grow after being confined in a pot for months.

Stir the soupy mix together with a shovel and then place the container into the hole to measure the depth. Make sure that the top of the root ball is at least as high as the original ground level. If you need to, add or remove material from the hole to make it the right height.

Now take the plant in its container out of the hole and roll the plant container along the ground while putting pressure on the sides of the container to loosen the root ball inside. Once the root ball is loosened from the pot, you can more easily pull it out of the container without damaging the roots or the tree itself.

Next hold the plant by the trunk near the root ball, and put the root ball into the hole. Hold the trunk of the tree, so that it is coming straight out of the ground (instead of at an angle). Then fill in around the root ball with your mulch and dirt mixture. Next, pack it down with your foot to get any air bubbles out.

Build a mound of soil at least 2 inches high on the outside edge of the hole to create a mini-berm to hold water. (You can use some of the clay that you may have dug out of the hole to do this. –It will retain water better than just topsoil.) If you are planting on the side of a hill, leave an opening on the uphill side, and a berm on the downhill side- which will make rain water stay with the plant longer and give it an opportunity to percolate down to the roots.

Cover any exposed dirt and the mound with decomposed mulch. Then soak the area around the planted tree with plain water. Fix any overruns, erosion, etc. that occur from pouring the water with more dirt, and more mulch. If your mini-berm doesn't work now, it won't work when it rains in the future. So pack it down and cover with mulch as needed.

Planting more than one plant in one hole- When planting several companion plants in a guild at the same time, here is a trick that can save you work and make your plantings work better: Instead digging a hole for each plant and then placing each plant in its own hole, we have come to plant multiple companion plants in one larger hole. In this situation the roots of these companion plants will mix and intertwine, share nitrogen, and work better together than they would by themselves

And planting symbiotic plants in the same hole is easier than digging multiple holes in the same area. Here is an example: You can plant a fruit tree, comfrey, Siberian Pea Shrub, and onions in a much larger hole using the same strategy of filling in the hole as outlined above.

Planting guilds- Start in zone one which you will remember is the zones closest to your home or the top elevation of your garden, and then work your way down, as you have time, plants and money to do so. For the time being you can let your lower zones go through pioneer stage until you are ready to plant them. This also creates a camouflaged border around your garden, since it will look like weeds have just overrun an open space.

Once you have your first zone planted, move on to zone 2, and improve on the process as you learn from your mistakes. If you start slow, you can then repeat your successes, as you expand your garden to include more guilds.

Plant your trees- The first plant to put in the ground in each guild should be your central guild tree- the fruit or nut tree that you are building each guild around. If you are planting multiple companion plants in one hole at the same time, plant your fruit tree with onions, garlic, Comfrey and a nitrogen fixing shrub, such as Siberian Pea shrub.

Give your fruit trees at least a 20 ft. diameter clear space from any other guild tree. This will allow trees to grow to maturity without branches hitting each other and without trees shading each other out.

Give your guild trees 20 ft. diameter of space from other guild trees.

If you assume that the branches on your mature fruit trees will extend out at least 10 ft. from the center of your tree, and if you assume that any other tree you plant next to it will do the same, you will need to leave at least 20 ft. of space in all directions between where you plant the trunk of each tree, in order to give them room to grow. Allowing even more space than 20 ft. also gives you room to plant shrubs (like blueberries and blackberries) around the drip-lines of the fruit trees.

Once you have planted the tree as in the section "How to Plant" (above), you may want to put a wire fence or cage around the new fruit trees as well as around your new shrubs (like blueberries). This fencing gives young plants the best chance for survival in a new garden, particularly if you have an area that was once a forest, where deer can continue to roam into your garden.

Keep in mind that it will also be less costly to fence around your individual trees, than it would be to fence in an entire garden, when you are just getting started.

I generally use a galvanized welded wire fence that is 5' tall and that is attached to itself in a 3-4 ft. diameter circle. This allows the tree's branches to grow up, where you can spread them out and train them to reach out over your berms after the branches reach 5' in height. Because deer can easily reach 4 ft. high to steal your fruit, you want your branches to start at 5' tall or higher. Also, you will want to be able to walk under the branches to pick from them, when the trees are mature so 5 ft. high is a good place to start.

Plant vines along-side trees. Grapes grow up trees in nature and grapes grow better climbing up trees than they do on man-made trellises.

Apple tree and grape vine planted together.

Grapes are a great fruit that can provide you with many valuable by-products. Aside from using grapes to make preserves, jellies, raisins and wines, you will need a source for making alcohol for both fuel and medicine in a long term survival situation. Fermenting grapes can give you that. By fermenting wine even further, grapes can provide you with vinegar, which can be used for preserving, cooking and even disinfecting kitchen and bath surfaces.

Plant shrubs around the perimeter of the drip line of the guild trees. Fruiting shrubs such as blackberries and blueberries contain valuable anti-oxidants; elderberries fights viruses. Make sure you plant in a way that leaves enough space between your shrubs and the future growth of your guild tree, so that the tree branches won't shade your bushes from the sun. Likewise allow for shrub expansion so that your fully grown shrubs do not crowd or shade the plants in your herb layer.

Using the same 5 ft. tall fencing that you used to cage your fruit trees, create 3 ft. diameter cages, to protect your berry bushes from deer, squirrels, raccoons and other animals that would like to eat your plants and your lunch (fruit). You also want to cover each metal cage with some additional plastic deer fence, particularly around the top of the fence.

The deer fencing is tightly woven enough to keep birds from flying down and taking your fruit before you can get to it, but the deer fence is also wide enough for bees and other pollinators to get in to pollinate your plants.

Blueberries and blackberries are part of your edible shrub layer.

Plant herbs- You can plant perennial herbs such as parsley, thyme and oregano for cooking, fever few for headache relief, echineacea to help with colds, lemon balm and mint for teas, mountain mint for clearing nostrils, and rosemary for cooking and repelling deer.

Herbs are medicine, add flavor to foods (to avoid food fatigue) and attract pollinators and good bugs that will prey on the bad bugs you don't want in your garden. For example, if you plant catnip around tomatoes, tomato horn worms won't go near it.

Mountain mint is also a great plant for attracting good bugs. It is fragrant and has more camphor than any plant I know. That's why it is great for clearing nostrils, if you have allergies or a cold. It is also a good medicine for your honey bees. The oils on this plant are carried back to the hive by worker bees, and these oils actually help to remove blood sucking mites that attach themselves to your bees.

Catnip and Mountain Mint are medicinal herbs that attract "good bugs".

When you are planting your herbs, leave space for growth of the herb and the plants around it (i.e. shrubs). Your herbs will expand over time and you will want to insure that they are not crowded, and do not also crowd other plants out.

Peach tree guild planted with herbs in front and berry bushes to the sides. Note that there is plenty of space between plants to allow them to grow.

Plant ground covers- Ground cover are plants that act like a green mulch and provide shade for the ground (to prevent evaporation) that have no other guild plants in it. Many of the ground covers are also nitrogen fixers or nutrient accumulators. Clover, vetch, dandelions, and even strawberries, can be planted outside of the herb layer and are effective and beneficial ground covers.

Since ground covers have a tendency to spread as they grow, you don't have to cover every square inch of empty space in your garden to cover the ground. You can also dig up ground covers later to plant other vegetables such as root crops and annual vegetables.

Plant strawberries for an edible, perennial ground cover.

Root crops- Root crops are crops where you eat the part that grows underground (as in the "roots"). Plants such as potatoes, sweet potatoes, and carrots, are common annual root crops that most people know. There are also perennial root crops (that you never have to replant) such as Jerusalem Artichokes (also known as Sunchoke), as well as Egyptian/walking onions, and others.

You can fill in between plants and between guilds with **perennial vegetables,** such as asparagus, and rhubarb.

When it comes to getting started with your permaculture food forest, you don't have to be overwhelmed. You don't have to plant everything all at once. Just plant a guild at a time, or a berm at a time. Start in zone 1, closest to home. Observe, observe, observe. See what works before expanding; then make adjustments and do it all over again. Notice hot spots, dry areas, wet areas, plant accordingly and continually improve.

Got wet areas? Then work with it. For example: plant cranberries and elderberries in the wet spots.

Annuals- Your typical annual vegetables can also be grown in among your permaculture guilds. Each spring you can plant your typical vegetables, from Arugula to Zucchini. But in keeping with the permaculture concept, it is best to mix and match and intersperse different plants in different places in each guild. Unlike row gardening, the other permaculture plants in each guild will provide more protection for your annual vegetables than planting vegetables in row gardens.

You can interplant annual vegetables with your perennial guilds.

You can also plant watermelon, pumpkin, squash, cucumbers and other vining annuals so that their vines run downhill the sides of your terraces. That way the long vines associated with these plants won't crowd out your other permaculture plantings and the vines will be able to run at will, getting light, rain and setting fruit.

Watermelon and other vining annuals can be planted to run down terraces.

Microclimates- Take advantage of the exposed rocks in your garden that heat up in the day and give off heat at night. Plant around them for a longer growing season. You can start harvesting sooner and your plants will bear fruit longer and later into the fall because they will be less apt to get hurt by early or late frosts.

Plant borders and "green fence"- As they say, out of sight out of mind. If you plant green vines along a fence you can disguise your garden from deer, raccoons, rabbits and people. If they don't see the plants you have growing there, they will not be interested in trying to breech your fence to get in.

By planting thorny runners like blackberries along your garden's borders or intertwining these plants along the side of a welded wire fence, also creates a green and prickly barrier that prevents animals like raccoons from climbing over. Since deer and people will take the path of least resistance, the more painful it looks to explore what they cannot see, the less likely they will attempt to see beyond the thorny vines.

CHAPTER 11
OBSERVING AND IMPROVING, NATURAL PEST CONTROL

Observe Water Flow- Now that your guilds are planted; note where puddles are and where overflows and erosion occurs. Build up areas that don't hold water with sticks, clay, and topsoil and keep piling the mulch on where needed.

Observe water flow, sun and shade, to make improvements as needed.

Observe Sun/ Heat/Shade- Plant your crops where they are most appropriate, to provide intense sun for plants that need it, or to provide shade for plants that need that. For example, I had two years of failing at growing dill, until a nursery man said- "You know these need shade don't you?" I had always planted my dill in full sun, just like my other herbs. So then I started planting dill on the north side of my fruit trees, and they did well!

Mulch more where needed. Look at bares spots created by water flow and keep areas covered to stop erosion and to prevent undue evaporation. ; tip- blueberries in particular like high acid- use pine needles as mulch

Compost- Learn to recycle and reuse organic matter for better use in your garden. Don't waste your potato peels, carrot shavings, and other food preparation scraps by throwing them in the trash. Instead keep a compost bucket by your food prep area, and empty it each evening into a composter. You can buy a plastic drum composter that allows you to add compost and soil into the drum. The drum heats up and helps to compost the contents faster as a result. Let it decompose and add the compost to the soil as nutrients.

Compost your kitchen scraps to add nutrients to your soil.

You can also use a compost bin that can be as simple as putting four small shipping pallets together to make four walls. You can add leaves, twigs, household scraps and other decomposable waste to this pile and you can turn it periodically with a pitchfork. You want your compost piles in the sun as well, but make sure your house windows are not down-wind of the pile, or you may end up smelling it when you open the windows.

Animal Compost- When cleaning out the stalls of your farm animals, their waste is mixed in with the straw or shavings in their pens (make sure they the shavings are not cedar because cedar doesn't break down well.)

The straw and the animal waste is a great combination that helps hold the soil in place and helps add nutrients to soil the "natural" way. Nature doesn't make artificial petrochemical fertilizers to put on soil- but nature sure does provide plenty of animal poop to do the job.

In nature, even animals' waste has a symbiotic relationship with the plants the animals eat. Animals benefit by eating the fruit, and the plant benefits by the animal releasing seeds of these digested plants from their bodies, and adding natural fertilizer to the soil (often surrounding the seed).

Straw mixed with waste from animal stalls, is great mulch that adds nutrients to the soil.

To take advantage of all this free fertilizer, just use a pitchfork to remove the straw/waste combination from the stalls. Then haul it to the plants on your berms in your wheelbarrow. Then use your pitchfork to evenly spread the straw on your terraces and around your plants. The straw also helps with the retention of water, the minimization of erosion and run-off, and adds great, nitrogen rich, non-chemical nutrients to the soil.

Pest Control:
I am often asked what I do about pests in my garden, since I am not using petro-chemical pesticides. For the most part, I let nature take care of

itself, and encourage good bugs, birds, lizards, spiders, and my ducks to eat up the bad bugs that I do not want to have in my garden.

But we also have pests, intruders, and down-right thieves that invade our garden that need to be controlled, if we are going to protect our investment. Here are some suggestions that work and that don't create more problems by poisoning your ground, your good bugs and other organisms that you need for a healthy garden.

Controlling 4 legged Pests:

Deer have been called "an appetite with 4 legs". Deer are creatures of habit, and if they get in the habit of going somewhere for food, it is hard to get them to stop. For example, if your garden happens to be cut out of an area of forest that had deer trails running through it, then the deer will still walk that way, and may venture into your garden. As soon as they discover that you have food planted there, they will keep coming back.

Before deer get started eating your crops there are things you can do to change their direction and to have them go around your garden, instead of travelling through it.

You can plant a "green fence" like Blackberries, Osage Orange, and bamboo along the borders of your garden that make it difficult for them to see, and difficult for them to get through. No one likes to get ripped open by thorns, so blackberries and Osage Orange are great plants to keep deer and other animals out.

Raccoons for example, look at a standard fence as if it was a ladder that you put there for them to climb into your garden. However if you put a green fence like blackberries along the border of a metal fence, these blackberries will be like razor wire hanging on the fence. Once the raccoons get torn up by the blackberries, they will probably let go of the fence, and find someplace else that will be a less painful source of food.

Rosemary and daffodil also repel deer. I have a friend who owns a plant nursery that is cut out of an old oak forest. Deer are abundant, but because deer don't like the smell of rosemary, they have made a path around his nursery, instead of through it.

Squirrels are just bushy tailed rats that will pilfer your strawberries, as well as any other fruits, nuts and vegetables that you have worked so have to get started. I had squirrels eating oat seeds as fast as I could plant them. As soon as I turned around and had walked 25 yards away, the squirrels were there grabbing the seed. However, if you sprinkle crushed Cayenne Pepper on the area that you are planting, the squirrels will get a whiff and taste of the pepper, and will steer clear after that.

Garlic, onions and chives will repel mice, and other rodents like rabbits. If you plant these around your important permaculture plants, you can keep mice from girding your tree in the winter.

A more extreme and stinky solution is a product commercially referred to as "Liquid Fence". You can buy this product for $15.00 per gallon, or you can simply make it yourself. All you need are eggs, garlic, hot pepper and water. To make it, find 5 one gallon milk or water jugs. Take one of the jugs and in it put 5 eggs (not cooked), a table spoon of crushed or minced garlic, a table spoon hot peppers, and fill the rest with water. Shake it up. Then split this mixture into equal portions in 4 other gallon milk jugs. Then fill each with water. Place caps on the jugs and set jugs in sun for 5-7 days. When it is ready it will be really stinky. Simply put this mixture in spray bottles and spray trees around your yard. Or, take the jugs and pour the mixture on the ground around the perimeter of your garden.

Lifebuoy soap- If you place lifebuoy soap in plastic bags and hang those around your garden, it will repel deer. (You put the soap in bags off the ground so that the soap won't get wet, but it still can give off its odor to repel deer.

Place Lifebuoy soap in plastic bags around your garden to deter deer.

Moth balls- Moth balls are a great pest deterrent. Moth balls not only deter moths, they also deter other creepy crawlers, as well as rodents.

In an outdoor survival situation, you can sprinkle moth balls around your camp site, and you won't have to worry as much about critters crossing the line into your camp. The same can be said for your garden. However, instead of throwing moth balls on the ground in your garden, you can put moth balls in plastic containers, and punch holes in those containers so that the smell can get out, but the poison can't get on the ground. This will also make the moth balls last longer (because they won't get wet in the rain).

Put these containers around the garden perimeter to keep the four legged pests out. I don't suggest that you put them near any plants that you want to have pollinated, as the moth balls will probably keep your pollinators away.

Punch holes in the side of plastic containers and put a few moth balls in the bottom to deter rodents from your garden.

CDs or DVDs hanging from a string will spin in the wind and the shiny surface will flash light. This will deter deer and some birds, but of course it defeats the camouflage effect of your garden. So in a grid down situation, you don't want such an obvious attention getter as flashing disks to highlight your forest garden.

Fishing line- If you string standard monofilament fishing line at 2 ft. above the ground, deer can't see it, and will walk into it at night. Feeling something against their legs spooks them, so they turn and run. Of course fishing line can break, so you have to monitor these strings on an ongoing basis.

Deer fence- Deer fence is an inexpensive thin woven plastic mesh, and like monofilament line it is almost invisible to deer and to humans. You can get deer fence that is 8 ft. tall, which is tall enough so deer won't jump over it. Just like fishing line, deer will walk into it and get spooked. However, it is not that strong and a deer can run through it if they get freaked out by getting tangled in it. Once they realize they can walk through it, you may have a problem with them getting into your garden.

Electric fence- An electric fence can use alternating current by connecting a transformer to a standard house external wall outlet. Of course, you have to be able to reach an outlet or a power cord to make this work. So that makes it difficult if your fence is not close to a 110v power source. It also assumes that you will always have electricity at your disposal, which may not be the case in a grid down situation. Another alternative is to use a solar charger that stores energy from the sun in a battery during the day and powers the electric fence continuously -24 hrs. per day.

Solar electric fence with one strand of wire, outside a welded wire fence.

You can use a single strand of electric wire to keep out animals like deer at about 2 ft. off the ground. Or can use 4 or 5 strands of wire that run parallel to each other at different heights. These wires can start at 6 inches off the ground and go to 5 ft. or more in height. Lower strands keep rabbits, and short animals out, as well as predators, i.e. foxes, etc. (most of which would rather dig under a fence than try to jump over it). The other wires will keep animals from stepping or jumping over the fence into your garden. Of course, you have to keep any live growth cleared around the perimeter of your fence so that lower strands won't come into contact with grass and other plants or they will short the electric charge and the fence won't keep anyone out.

You can "teach" deer, raccoons, squirrels, etc. to stay away from your garden by putting peanut butter on a small square of aluminum foil and then folding that aluminum foil over the "hot" electric wire of your fence. Deer are attracted to the smell of peanut butter, and when they go to have a taste, they get a little more flavor than they bargained for. Experiencing this once or twice and they will steer clear of your fence and garden forevermore.

One more note on electric fencing, make sure you have good grounding rod(s) driven deep into the ground to attach your ground wire to. If your fence is not well grounded, your hot wire may not have much effect.

Chain Link- Chain link is strong, but very expensive. In fact, most experts will tell you that the best fence you can buy to protect a garden would be an 8 ft. tall chain-link fence. If the fence is embedded in the ground this will keep most animals out, including predators such as fox as well as most bear. The exception to this is the raccoon who acts like fences are a ladder you put there especially for him to climb over. If you add barbed wire (or even better- razor wire) jutting out at a 45 degree angle over the top of the fence (like you see in prisons), this will keep animals like raccoons (and people) from climbing over.

If you can't afford chain link, but still want to put a perimeter fence all around your garden, you can do that with 5' to 6' galvanized welded wire fence. It's not as strong as chain link- but it will stop most creatures- and you can disguise it from humans by growing green vines and blackberry bushes along it. This will not only disguise it the fence, but it will also keep people and critters from climbing over if they happen to find it.

Fire Ant Pest Control- Fire ants are becoming an ever increasing problem, and there is nothing much worse than picking fruit from your trees, and suddenly having your leg covered with fire ants. Additionally fire ants kill the good ants in your garden, and those good ants provide benefits to you by preying on bad bugs and by loosening soil that allows water to penetrate and roots to grow.

Fire ants can be killed with boiling water or corn meal.

Using fire ant killers, like any pesticide, create unwanted side-effects in your permaculture garden. These chemicals not only kill fire ants, but they can also kill the microbes in your soil, as well as the good bugs, and lizards, etc. that work to keep the other pests down in your garden.

Here are some less poisonous and more natural ways to get rid of fire ants on your property.

Boiling Water- You can cook up a gallon pot of plain old boiling water on your stove, and while it is steaming hot, pour it right down on the colony. The water will penetrate the colony and cook the ants. And if you are lucky, you will kill the queen, which will then kill the colony.

Corn meal- This takes a little longer but is effective. If you put corn meal on the mound, the ants will bring it down into the colony and will gorge on it. The ants can't digest the corn meal so when the ants eat it they basically get a bad case of constipation and they die.

Boric Acid- Just like using Borax in your home to kill cock roaches, fire ants will also die if you put boric acid around the colony. The ants get the boric acid on their bodies and since they absorb oxygen through their pores, the borax gets in their pores and they are then unable to breathe. The problem with boric acid is that it also kills good bugs and microbes in the soil.

Fire ants on fire ants- If you are bored on the farm and are looking for some grid-down entertainment, you can start fire ant wars and watch them battle against each other. Simply grab a shovel full of ants and dirt from one mound and place it on top of another fire ant mound. The fire ants will fight to the death, and will not only kill each other, but if you are lucky, the "invading" ants will kill the queen from the other colony, thus killing that colony altogether.

(If you have two people, each with a shovel, you can double your fun by doing two colonies at once!)

Aphids, and other creepy crawlies- If you have a greenhouse, and are growing plants during the winter, or early spring and late fall, there will be no natural predator insects available to control an aphid population.

We had planted 400 seedlings (mostly annual vegetables) in small pots in our greenhouse when there was still frost outside. We wanted the plants to have a good head start, so that they would be ready to plant in the spring. What we had not anticipated was that aphids were in the soil of the greenhouse, and with no natural predators available, the aphids multiplied so fast that the stems of our green seedlings looked white from their tiny bodies as they literally sucked the life out of our plants. We knew we had to do something – and fast. And then we discovered tomato leaves.

Tomato leaves- What do you do with the leaves of tomatoes when the plant dies off at the end of the summer season? Most people don't do anything but turn them back into the soil. However you can do something better- just save the leaves and dry them. Keep them in a paper bag in a dark dry area, and in a save them for the future.

The alkaloids in the tomato leaves miraculously kill aphids! All you have to do is steep the dried leaves in hot water overnight, then take the green fluid and put it in a spray bottle. Spray the solution on the aphids. It won't hurt plants or soil.

CHAPTER 12
GROWING THROUGH THE SEASON

Now that you have your guilds planted, your annuals planted in between, and you have your natural pest control in place, all you have to do now is watch in amazement, as nature does what it does best, and your plants, insects, lizards, and other garden creatures work in harmony to raise your crops for you.

Plants blooming at different times, keep good bugs coming all the time.

Bloom times- Because you have planted using permaculture concepts, you will have plants that are early bloomers, late bloomers and bloom throughout the season in between. This is great if you have honey bees, because they will be feeding constantly, and making healthy honey for you.

Your other pollinators will be hanging around your garden throughout the growing season too. This means that you will have natural pest controlling helpers for *all* the plants in your garden.

When you consider planting trees and shrubs, it is always best to have two of the same type of plant in your garden that will bloom at the same time for crosspollination. Even though many plants today are "self-pollinating", you will have more success and more fruit, if you have more than one tree of the same type. For example, you should have two peach trees, two fig trees, two pear trees, etc. (It is even better if you have three of each type.)

You don't have to plant all of your cross pollinating trees next to each other. In fact, it is actually better if you don't. That way the bad bugs don't attack the same type of plants without having to travel across the yard. In the meantime, the bad bugs can be thwarted by predator bugs before they can devastate one crop. Likewise, if you have two trees blooming at the same time that are across the yard from each other, your pollinators are likewise forced to fly across your garden, which gives them a greater chance of running into the bad bugs you want them to prey on.

Keep in mind that some of the same kind of fruit trees actually blossom and set fruit at different times of the year. For example, early blooming apples and late blooming apples won't cross pollinate because they bloom at different times.

Harvest times –One of the great things about permaculture is that not all of your plants are ripe at the same time. So you can handle the harvesting work load. Just like different fruit trees will bloom at different times, different fruit will usually bear fruit at different times.

In our area, we harvest strawberries first, then come blackberries, apricots, nectarines, peaches, plums, grapes, pears, apples, figs, passion fruit, chestnuts, peanuts, etc.

Since not all your fruit is harvested at the same time, you have time to process that fruit, by preserving, dehydrating, etc. Although, even that can be difficult given the success of plants in a permaculture garden. Less than 2 years after we started our garden, I was bringing in at least a 3 gallon bucket per day of fruit. That's a lot of canning on a day to day basis.

Ever-bearing strawberries are an example of a plant that produces more than just one round of fruit in the season. Ever-bearing strawberries bear a big crop early in the season and then continue to grow, blossom, and bear fruit throughout the summer and late into fall. In fact, I have had strawberries maturing as late as Thanksgiving, even after several morning frosts.

Ever-bearing Strawberries provide fruit throughout the growing season.

Another benefit of using permaculture gardening is that plants typically have a longer bearing season than what most people are used to. Most people have their tomato plants done and pulled out of the ground by mid-summer. Whereas, I have tomatoes growing into November, until night temperature gets to below 40 degrees. And thermal mass like cement walls, stones, etc. can keep growing season even longer.

Tomatoes, watermelon, peppers and sweet potatoes in November!

Weeds-I have said before that weeds are just misunderstood plants. As permaculture gardeners we need to learn to love and appreciate them. Weeds are pioneer plants and make the soil better. They grow where there are not enough nutrients for other plants to grow, and when they die they decompose and make way for other plants.

And when many plants are already done

for the season, certain weeds are still going strong, blossoming and creating nourishment for the honey bees and other pollinators that will protect your year-end crops from the bad bugs before you can harvest them.

Weeds are just misunderstood plants. Weeds often grow when nothing else will, and they provide food for bees, when all your other plants are at seasons end.

Mushrooms- Mushrooms can grow in a shaded area that is not being used by other plants in your cleared space. You can grow mushrooms by taking some of the hardwood trees that you felled when clearing your property and stacking the trees so that are off the ground- in sort of an A-frame. This allows you to harvest mushrooms under the trees as well.

You can harvest mushrooms from your Secret Garden of Survival as well.

Since so many mushrooms are poisonous, and since so many look similar, it is best for you to buy an "inoculation kit" of mushroom plugs so that you will know what type of mushrooms you are actually growing.

All you need to do is drill small holes into the trees and insert the plugs in the drilled holes.

Training vines- As the season goes on, and particularly as the season comes to a close, you should "train" your vining plants to go where you want them to go, and not necessarily everywhere that they want to go.

By training, trimming and otherwise managing vining plants you can avoid some plants blocking out sunlight of other guild plants. Blackberries in particular have root system that spread, so you can have blackberries where you don't want them. When that happens they will shade out your other plants, berries, etc. I dig up the ones that are growing where I did not plant them, and if I can get enough of the root, I plant these blackberries along the fence, for a green and thorny barrier for my garden, that also bears fruit.

Likewise there are plants in your food forest that need to have not only open sun, but also airflow, blueberries, for example. That is why blueberries will do well planted at the top of a berm, where they can get light and a gentle breeze.

Any trimmings that you cut from plants that you are trying to manage can simply be thrown on the ground. Just let these branches and sticks decompose where they lie. They will create mulch and nutrients that will make the rest of your garden stronger.

Drop trimmings on the ground to decompose, adding nutrients to the soil.

Likewise you will want to trim your fruit trees after they start losing their leaves in the fall, so that branches grow in the direction you want them to grow. (You don't want a bunch of branches crossing each other or keeping sun and air flow from the inside center of the tree.) Those trimmings can also be used as mulch. Or apple and pear branches make particularly good chew sticks for your rabbit livestock. (They will thank you for it.)

End of the 1st season- At the end of your first season you can sit back and congratulate yourself, because you now have the beginning of your own Secret Garden of Survival. Your plants and guilds should be starting to take shape, and you will even have harvested some fruit from some of your plants.

5 months after starting with red clay; the end of the 1st season of planting.

You only need to do a little work preparing your guild plants for next year by trimming, pruning and training vines and branches so they will start growing where you want them to next season.

Mulching barren areas with more decomposed mulch or straw/animal waste from your livestock stalls will protect the soil from wind, water, and snow erosion when there are no green plants covering the ground.

The following year your plants should take on a life of their own, and you will be amazed at how fast and how well they grow. The plants will expand in height and width and the garden will fill in. Your Secret Garden of Survival will begin looking more like a forest, and there will be less distinguishing features for specific plants.

In fact, you will spend very little time worrying about your plants growing, and far more time worrying about them growing too much.

The majority of your work now will be harvesting your crops, every day or every couple of days. As with anything else, observe, and improve as you learn and as you expand into your outer zones.

After two growing seasons- After two growing seasons your food forest should be fully filled out and in many ways it will be indistinguishable as anything but an overgrown open area in the middle of a timber forest. If anyone happened upon it, it would not look like it was any sort of "garden" at all.

Upon close inspection, they would see that there was food everywhere, but if they can't tell that from a distance, then they won't have any interest in looking closer at what appears to be an overgrown field.

Blackberries blossoming in a fully filled out food forest.

Just for your encouragement, I offer you the following photos of the original Secret Garden of Survival, after only two growing seasons. We started with red clay in March, and a year and a few months later, we had a lush, natural looking food forest.

Food Forest after only two growing seasons.

I have been amazed at how well nature works, if you let nature do what nature wants to do, and keep from interfering with the natural order of things. The growth of our Secret Garden of Survival has been nothing short of phenomenal, and our harvests after only two growing seasons provided us with more food than we can dehydrate, preserve, and consume.

Before and After

Red clay to 12 ft. high blackberry bushes in only 2 years.

Red clay to a lush food forest in only 2 years.

Good luck with your own Secret Garden of Survival and be looking for our website, newsletter, tips and twitter feeds on how to do even more with your new food forest.

-BONUS CHAPTER-
WHAT TO DO AFTER THE HARVEST

After you start harvesting your crops, you should have an abundance of food from your Secret Garden of Survival, and it should produce more than you can consume at the time you harvest. That's a good thing. You want to have more than you can eat right now. But once you pick it, your fruit and vegetables will start to decompose, some faster than others. It's just nature's way.

Thus, you need to consider what you will do with your abundance, so that you can survive for a year, until the next harvest of each particular fruit or vegetable.

For centuries, people have stored and preserved foods in a number of ways, from pickling, to salting, to canning, to dehydrating. Today most people in the modern world use a refrigerator and a freezer, but these appliances have not been around for very long, and in a grid down situation, these electric devices will be useless.

Unfortunately, it has been less than 100 years, but in our age of consumerism and convenience, we have lost the art and knowledge of food preservation without electricity. Yet people all over the world, survived from year to year, for thousands of years, because they knew how to do it.

Since we don't have a lot of space to go into a great deal of depth in this book, we will be putting out another book soon that will go into detail about Survivalist Food Preservation.

For now we will discuss some basics of the many ways you can preserve your harvest from your Secret Garden of Survival.

Save seeds- Many of your fruits and vegetables have seeds within the part that you eat. Many of these seeds can be used for far more than just planting new crops. For example, Muscadine Grape seeds may not be something you would eat in the process of eating the grapes, and most of the time the seeds are removed when you are making jellies and other preserves from grapes. However, you can save and dry Muscadine Grape seeds, and then you can grind them up into a fine powder and sprinkle this as a condiment on other foods. The Muscadine seeds have strong anti-carcinogenic properties, so this is a medicine as well.

Many of your other seeds have similar properties and can be used for purposes beyond just food. Do some research, and see what you can use other seeds for.

Many seeds are just plain good food, and seeds and nuts are a part of a good balanced survival diet. Sunflower seeds can be eaten as is, or made into oil that can be sued for cooking. Peanuts can be eaten, as is, roasted, made into peanut oil, and made into peanut butter. Roasted and salted pumpkin seeds are always a favorite and almost make putting your hands inside the pumpkin to separate the seeds from the stringy pulp, worth the effort.

Of course many people want to save the seeds from their fruits and vegetables to use for replanting next year. This is a good idea, but you also need to understand what it is that you are saving, because you can waste a lot of time and effort saving seeds that will never sprout, or that may sprout and never bear fruit.

Once you have your established perennial permaculture plants growing, you probably won't be saving peach or apple seeds for starting new trees right away. However, most people will need to collect seeds from their annual vegetables in order for there to be any crop whatsoever the following season.

Grow Heirloom Seeds and Plants. Wherever possible, you want to grow and store heirloom seeds. Heirloom seeds are seeds that have been around before man started messing with them, and they grow vegetables that are true to their heritage. Heirloom seeds are harder to find these days, although at one time, heirlooms were all that existed.

Grow Non-GMO seeds and plants. GMO stands for Genetically Modified Organism. And this means what it says. Man (scientists) that work for the big chemical and agricultural companies have genetically modified what were once nature's plants. By splicing genes into these plants, they create sometimes bigger, more disease and pest resistant plants than the natural plants.

Although at first this may seem like a good thing, it is not. Some of the genes that they splice into these plants, don't' necessarily come from the same species- and some don't even come from plants. In fact some come from animals! That's like taking some of your genes, and splicing them with genes from a plant, to create your next child.

Additionally these GMO's are patented, so that no one else can manufacture them, and so that no one else can grow them, without paying the inventing company (i.e. Monsanto) for the right to do so.

And many of these GMOs are intentionally sterile, so even if they do produce seeds, their seeds will not sprout or will not produce more fruit. This is in no small way, part of a corporate monopoly strategy to control the world's food supply. (If you control the seeds, then you control the food supply.)

Whether you subscribe to that "conspiracy theory" or not, rest assured that you are wasting your time planting GMO crops if you think you will be able to save the seeds and replant them to grow more crops the following year.

Grow Non-Hybrid Seeds and Plants. Hybrid plants are not necessarily genetically modified, and they are often just a cross between to plants of the same species, but with different attributes. Hybrids can be created naturally by simple cross pollination between two similar plants. So for example, two different varieties of tomatoes can be cross pollinated by a bee, giving you a tomato that has qualities of both parent tomatoes. This could be a good or a bad thing.

The problem with hybrids, is that you know what you are going to get when you plant the seed the first time- but you don't necessarily know what you will get in the next generation, or then next one after that. So simply put, if you plant a hybrid tomato and save the seeds for next year, when you plant those seeds, you may not get the same tomato that they came from.

So for the sake of argument, let's assume that you take my advice and that you plant heirloom seeds and plants. Designate a few plants that you will let go to seed. For example, plants like carrots have seed pods that flower and then create seeds. If you pick and eat the carrots when they are ripe, you will never be able to collect seeds to plant next year.

For plants that have seeds growing inside them, picking plants before they go to seed makes them more productive- especially in the case of vegetables like peas and beans. Because the plant wants to procreate before the summer is over, if you pick the vegetables before it goes to seed, it keeps trying to make seeds. This actually makes these plants produce more food for you. Once the summer is almost over, save some plants that are doing well, and designate them as your seed plants. Then let those beans or peas (for example) dry up on the vine, so that you can then keep those hardened seeds for next year's plantings.

Saving herbs. You have been growing herbs as part of your Secret Garden of Survival and you have probably been using the leaves as part of your cooking or medicines as they have grown throughout the summer. You probably have added oregano to spaghetti, or mint to teas, and picked these herb leaves as you needed them. However, as the summer draws to a close, you will want to pick and store leaves for use throughout the winter (until you can gather new leaves from these herbs in the spring).

Most herbs can be saved quite simply by taking the leaves off the plant before the first frost. You can then dry the leaves in a paper bag by loosely closing the top of the bag. Use a marker to write on the outside of the bag in order to label the type of herb that is in the bag. Store the dried leaves in a cool dry place (like your pantry). When the leaves are dry you can crumble them up, and use them for cooking or simply put them in a shaker, and use them to sprinkle on food.

You can also use certain herbs to make tinctures with alcohol; for medicinal purposes.

Food Storage in the ground- When it comes to storing root crops, such as potatoes, sweet potatoes, turnips, beets, carrots, etc. often the best place to store these crops is right in the ground. At the end of the season, their green tops or vines fall off and decay, leaving the root crop in the ground. They can store quite well there, as long as no animal digs them up.

The only problem with doing this in a permaculture concept is that unless you mark these plants with flags for digging up in the winter when you need them, you are going to have a tough time finding them out there in the garden. (This is the one instance where row planting would make it easier for you to find your crops in the off season, since all your similar plants would be planted in the same row.)

One solution is to store these root crops in dirt mounds outside of your home. You simple dig up the potatoes, for example, and you place them in a mound of dirt with your other potatoes, so that when you need to get a couple of potatoes for dinner, you can go out to the mound and find some.

Root Cellar- Much like storing food in a mound or in the ground, a root cellar is a great place to store root crops (thus the term "root cellar").

Interestingly enough, almost every farm had a root cellar specifically for that purpose. A root cellar was basically a big hole in the dirt, with a house or a roof on top. The root cellar worked as a storage area because being underground, so it was dark, it maintained a constant temperature of about 55 degrees (so it was cool in the summer and did not freeze in the winter) and because it was underground, it maintained a fairly high humidity. All of these qualities made a root cellar perfect for storing root crops. It was also a good place for storing other foods as well.

The root cellar was so important to a family farm, that it was often the first building that a new homestead built. The family often slept in the root cellar until they could finish the other buildings on the farm. (The next building was the barn for the animals, and the last building was the house for the people. –See how they had their priorities straight?)

The following is a list of some of the food that should be stored in a root cellar:

Apples – Will keep for 5-8 months. (Apples give off a gas, that makes root vegetables sprout or spoil, so store apples in separate spaces from your other root crops). Apples also like to be moist so store in a barrel lined with paper or sawdust.

Cabbage - Will keep for 3-4 months. Place in plastic bags that have holes to let excess moisture escape.

Celery - Will keep 2-3 months.

Hot peppers- Will keep for 6 months.

Pears will keep for 3 months. Pack in loose papers in crates and barrels.

Root crops- Potatoes (5-8mos), beets (3mos), turnips (4-5mos) - You can put all of these in separate crates of clean sand. Keep out of any light.

Carrots and parsnips will keep 4-6 months. Snip off the tops just above the crown and store in covered containers filled with moist sand.

You can build a root cellar into your existing house. This is especially true if you have a basement area. Just frame out a small room that is 5 feet wide so that you have room to walk between 18 inch shelves on either wall. Insulate the walls and ceiling from the heat in the house (so it will remain cool inside the root cellar.) If you have casement windows in the basement, you can have a 2" pipe coming into the root cellar to bring in cool fresh air, and have that pipe extend to the floor. (Cold air sinks.) Since hot air rises, have a vent at the top of the room that exits air to the outside. This simple pipe and vent will give your room circulation and keep it cool, when you need it to be cool the most, after your harvest and into the spring.

Pantry- A pantry can be a small cabinet or a big closet that is dark and has shelves for storage. In your case, you may want to consider making a big closet, since you are going to have a lot of harvest you will need to store.

A pantry is generally used to store dry goods like bulk sugar, flour, spaghetti, rice, etc. since a pantry is generally warmer and drier than a root cellar. A pantry is also a great place to store your canned goods (both store bought and those that you have canned yourself) since the low humidity keeps cans and their metal covers from rusting.

Aside from canned products you can also store onions that will last 8 months as well as Garlic that will last 7 months. Just pull them out of ground when tops fall over and begin to dry. When tops are completely dry, cut them off 1 inch from the bulbs. Cure them for another week. Then keep them dry and stored in mesh bags or crates.

A pantry is the place to store canned goods, pumpkins, and grains.

Hot peppers can be stored for 6 months in a pantry. You can hang the peppers up by stringing a thread through the top part of each pepper and then hanging them in the air to dry.

Pumpkins will last 3months and squash will keep for 6 months. Just make sure that you leave part of stem on them when you cut them from the vine, and of course, keep them dry.

When setting up your pantry make certain that you have strong shelves and that the wall supports are strong as well. You will have a lot of weight on these shelves and the last thing you want to have happen is to have glass canning jars smashing to the ground, losing a year's worth of preserves, soups, beans, and other harvests because your shelves couldn't hold the weight. (This goes double if you happen to be concerned with potential earthquakes in your area.)

Freezing- Freezing has become the modern world's solution to storing food. Everyone has a freezer, and we store our frozen vegetables, fruits, meat, and other food products in our freezers. We get our food frozen from the store, and we keep it frozen until we need it. We even store the left-overs and extras in the refrigerator or the freezer after we cook it.

One problem with relying on a freezer is that you can't keep a year's worth of food that you harvest from your forest garden, in a freezer. It just will not be enough space. You would need several large freezers to do so.

And most freezers run on electricity (some run on propane). Not only is it costly to run a freezer (or several), but what are you going to do if you lose electricity for a day or more? You would lose all your storage food and potentially a year's worth of food. Furthermore, in a long term grid down situation, there is not going to be any electricity nor will there be any more propane deliveries.

Store food in freezers until you can dehydrate or can your harvests.

My suggestion is that you use freezing as a short term solution to preserving your harvests, until you can preserve your various fruits and vegetables in some other way (i.e. by canning, dehydrating, pickling, etc.).

For example, when our grapes were ripening, I was bringing in over 6 gallons of grapes per day. This went on for weeks. That would have been an insurmountable amount of jellies and jams to be canning in typical Ball canning jars every day. So to make things easier, we put what we couldn't can in a day into the freezer for processing later.

Canning- Canned goods were not always food processed in sealed metal cans. In fact, in the scheme of things, manufactured canned goods are a very recent phenomenon. Most of you reading this book had a grandmother or great grandmother that used to can her own fruits in glass jars to make jellies and jams. In fact, our modern grocery term for "preserves" comes from the old meaning of preserved food. Now it has come to mean almost exclusively fruit condiments called "jam".

The difference between jelly and jam is that jellies are made strictly from syrup created from the fruit, whereas jams are made with the syrup and the fruit pieces as part of the end product in the jar. So jellies are made with the fruit syrup only, and jams or "preserves" have fruit in them.

There are basically two kinds of canning for our purposes. One is the water bath method, and the other is the pressure canning method.

Water bath canning uses boiling water and places your canning jars with your fruit, syrup or whatever contents you have, into a boiling hot water bath. The heat cooks out any germs that might contaminate your food. Once you put the hot lid on the top of the glass jar, a vacuum seal is created between the glass jar and the lid. Thus, the sterile jar remains sterile and the contents inside are "preserved".

Canning is an excellent way to preserve your harvests.

Water bath canning is used for contents that usually have a high sugar content, like fruits, etc. and is the simplest form of canning.

Pressure canning is used for foods that have a higher fat content, (or not a high sugar content). Pressure canning allows the water bath to get to a temperature higher than 212 degrees F, because the contents are under pressure in a pressure canner. Therefore certain vegetables and meats that would not be safe to can in a simple water bath can preserved in this way.

Dehydrating-Of all preserving methods, dehydrating is one of my favorites.

Dehydrating basically removes water from the food, so that bacteria and other contaminants can't live in it. Dehydrating is like drying the food in the sun. Dehydrating doesn't "cook" the food like you would in an oven, because it is done over a longer time and at a lower temperature.

You can dehydrate all kinds of foods, from corn kernels, to apple sauce. You can dehydrate tomato paste, and turn it into a powder, that can then be stored and rehydrated (simply adding water back to it) when you need it.

Since most any food's volume is taken up by water, dehydrated food takes less space, weighs less, and also doesn't use as many canning jars.

Therefore, dehydrating is also less expensive and you are less apt to lose food to broken glass from earthquake, storm, etc., or simply have shelves falling down from excess weight. For example, a 5 lb. bag of frozen corn can be dehydrated down to fit into a small sandwich bag. And when you want to eat it, you simply put the corn back in water, and it will rehydrate to its original size and texture, without any loss in flavor.

Dehydrating preserves food by removing water, reducing size and weight.

Dehydrated food is also easy to carry in a bug out situation, since it is lightweight and takes up far less space in a back pack.

You don't necessarily have to rehydrate it to eat it either. Many of these foods can be eaten as is. However, be careful about eating it without rehydrating, because dehydrated food still contains the same number of calories even though it has very little volume. So in our 5 lb. bag of corn example, you could easily eat the equivalent of a whole 5 lb. bag of corn in one sitting by consuming a mere sandwich bag of dehydrated corn. So the moral is, be careful, because you can eat a lot of calories without realizing it.

You can store dehydrated foods in the open, in plastic bags, or for the longest shelf life, you can store the food in vacuum sealed canning jars.

CONCLUSION

Before and after photos. Red clay to a lush food forest in only 2 years.

Now you know how to create your own Secret Garden of Survival.

This garden will help you to survive after your food stores run out- and it will disguise your garden and your food from the hordes from who would otherwise consume it after the fit hits the shan.

You will have a survival food garden that provides all the fruit, veggies, nuts and berries that you and your family can consume. You will only have to plant it once, you never have to fertilizer or use pesticide, and you can harvest your food for a lifetime.

Good luck with your own Secret Garden of Survival and check out our website, newsletter, and all our social media, for tips on how you can do even more, with your new food forest. (See all the links on page 111.)

-The Survivalist Gardener

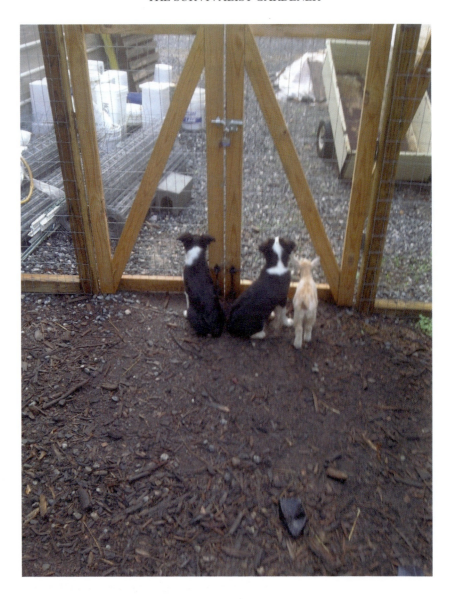

The End(s)

CONTACT INFORMATION

You can contact Rick Austin, the Survivalist Gardener and get information, ask questions and get tips and tricks, simply by following him through any of these resources:

Survivalist Gardener Website and Social Media Links:

Website: www.SecretGardenofSurvival.com
(Sign up for my weekly Newsletter!)

Facebook: www.facebook.com/SecretGardenOfSurvival

Twitter: www.twitter.com/SurvivorGarden   (@SurvivorGarden)

Google+: http://plus.google.com/+SurvivalistGardner

Linkedin: www.linkedin.com/in/survivalistgardener

YouTube: http://www.youtube.com/survivalistgardener

Pintrest: www.pintrest.com/SurvivorGarden

Secrets of a Survivalist Radio Show:

http://www.preparednessradio.com/shows/secrets-of-a-survivalist-rick-austin/

MORE CONTACT INFORMATION

For consulting, speaking engagements, or other information send us an email at SurvivorGarden@att.net .

To subscribe to our Secret Garden of Survival™ Newsletter, just fill in your email address at www.SecretGardenOfSurvival.com . By subscribing to our newsletter you will receive timely tips throughout the year on planting and managing your own Secret Garden of Survival™.

Or follow us on Twitter, Facebook, LinkedIn, Google+, YouTube, Pintrest and other social media.

Be looking soon for our other books on:

Secret Greenhouse of Survival- How to Build the Ultimate Homestead & Prepper Greenhouse

Secret Livestock of Survival- Raising Animals for Sustainable Living

Secret Food Preservation of Survival;
Secret Pond and Grey Water System of Survival,
Secret Rainwater Collection Systems of Survival,
Secret Root Cellar and Bunker of Survival

ABOUT THE AUTHOR
(OK-SO IT IS ALL ABOUT ME.)

Rick Austin is known as the Survivalist Gardener, and is a preparedness and off grid living expert. He is the author of **Secret Garden of Survival- How to Grow a Camouflaged Food Forest** which within nine months of its release, became the #1 Best Selling book in Garden Design.

And he is the author of the **Secret Greenhouse of Survival- How to Build the Ultimate Homestead & Prepper Greenhouse**.

Rick has also been featured on National Geographic Channel's **Doomsday Castle** and **Doomsday Preppers**, as well as the documentary film **Beyond Off Grid** and in **Mother Earth News**.

For more info and for all his social media links, go to his website: www.SecretGardenOfSurvival.com

You can also hear Rick on his radio show **Secrets of a Survivalist** where each week he talks with the world's best survival experts that share their own secrets of survival.

http://www.preparednessradio.com/shows/secrets-of-a-survivalist-rick-austin/